Although everything in this book is true, some of the names of people and places have been changed for discretionary reasons.

To Aaron,

To my best hockey buddy.
May this book assist you
in your happiness journey!

This book is dedicated to Arathi Ma.

ISBN: 978-1-257-93940-4

Acknowledgments

Much of my life has been an unconventional journey. One writer of anthropological works, Joseph Campbell, said that his journey through his youth was different than most. He called himself a Maverick. Well, I wish I could paint the escapades of my search for myself in such a positive light. Let's just say that I have enough material for a prequel to this story. I wish to give thanks to those that stood by me during part or all of my journey.

Thank you to:

Sean Sommerville, for teaching me everything I know about writing – I have much more to learn.

My parents, for standing by me through the barroom brawls of my youth, for supporting me during my depression and my aggressive ways of dispelling it, for accepting the fact that your son was never going to be like everyone else, and most importantly, for loving me no matter what.

My brother, Jamie, for introducing me to Arathi Ma. Without a stubborn-ass brother like him, I would never have conceded to seeing Arathi Ma. I also wish to thank him for being my most enthusiastic advocate in every hair-brained endeavor I embarked upon. He has my eternal thanks. Jamie, I love you...no matter what.

Tara, for giving birth to my niece, Deyva, and for witnessing the many challenging moments of my journey...and feeding me through all of it.

Everyone, who encouraged me to put my journey down on paper so that I could share it with the world.

Thomas-Ashley Farrand, for giving me the tools to start my journey towards Realization and for showing me what true humility looked like.

All spiritual seekers, for having the courage to follow the path less travelled.

Arathi Ma, for showing me every miracle imaginable, for giving me unconditional love, for waiting impatiently for every chapter of this book, and for her continual guidance and patience with me as I struggled to put her teachings into practice.

Foreword

It is my firm belief that the sharing of one's spiritual path has a healing effect on everyone gracious enough to listen. I wish to extend my gratitude to you for your open hearts and minds. My path was my own. It may not be for everyone, but my highest hope is that by reading the words in the pages ahead that a tool or realization is revealed to you and that it aids you on your path to true happiness. A world full of happy people would be a much different place indeed.

I also wish to share the fact that the opinions expressed in the book were mine at the time of the events, and although many of my opinions remain the same, many have changed as I have evolved. The purpose of this book is to take you with me as I travelled my spiritual path, so it was necessary for reasons of authenticity to give you my feelings, opinions, and personality as it was at any given time, not how it is at the time of writing this book.

If you examine the upcoming pages closely, you may be able to find patterns that resonate with your own existence. You may not be meditating, chanting mantras, or praying with fervor, but as many great sages have said, "Your entire life is a spiritual experience." The fact that you have even attempted to read this book says that some part of you is searching for your true self.

Continue forward. You will find it.

Beginnings

A long, black-haired, middle-aged woman sat with me at a small, two-person table. She was a nice-looking lady, and didn't have the stereotypical appearance of the latest psychics appearing on television.

Irene shuffled the Tarot cards, apparently deciphering the meaning.

"You're a difficult one to read," she said.

"I hear that a lot," I said, twisting in my seat to get comfortable. My butt just never fit onto a wooden chair properly. No matter which way I shifted, it seemed like the wood dug straight into a sore muscle or bone.

Irene looked up from the cards. "Someone is here. You had a friend that passed away a few years ago." The table lamp flickered, as if to accentuate her message.

I didn't answer, wondering if this psychic was fishing for information, or if she was the real deal.

Irene closed her eyes. "He's showing me head trauma. He died suddenly."

She was right. A friend of mine named Densel had died three years earlier in a motorcycle accident.

I grew eager to speak to him. Densel had been a great friend, and although he died in his early twenties, he had the humility of a senior citizen despite his good looks and charisma. "Does he have a message for me?"

Irene's eyes flickered. "Acorns."

I leaned forward. "What did you say?"

Irene shook her head and shrugged. "He's saying, 'Acorns.' I don't know what it means."

I searched my memory for the meaning, but found nothing. I couldn't remember a single time in our friendship where the word "acorn" was exchanged.

Irene must have seen the confusion on my face. "You have some questions?"

"You mean, besides what does the word 'Acorns' mean?"

She frowned and tilted her head, her frustration with the lack of information apparent in her expression. "Don't worry about it now. In time, the meaning of the message will come to you."

I shook my head, puzzling over Densel's message. I paid Irene the money for the session and then perused the books in her store. There were many books on Tarot reading, on spirituality of all traditions, but one particular book stood out to me the most. The cover held a picture of a beautiful tiger walking through a pond. Something about the way its green eyes gazed outward from the glossy cover enchanted me. I read the first few pages and found that the book contained a series of shamanic meditations in order to change one's life.

I bought the book and went home to read it. I didn't have much else happening these days, my girlfriend had dumped me, and I had recently quit my job. Life had disassembled before my eyes, and I had few friends or anything else to occupy my time. My social life had been reduced to playing hockey a few times a week and a regular daily visit to the gym.

The conversation with my ex girlfriend kept coming back to me over and over. She had said, "I just don't see you going anywhere, or doing anything. Nothing makes you happy and you're always depressed."

I didn't really have an answer for her. She spoke the truth. Depression had slithered into my life like a serpent and once it had me in its grip, there was no escaping from it.

"I know. I don't know how to be happy," I said, feeling horrible about it. I was frustrated with how I felt, but I didn't know how to change it.

My girlfriend sighed. "I can't stand it anymore. I want to do things and you're never going to be ready for them, so there's no point in us being together."

I nodded, my self-hatred growing with her every word. "I know."

We had parted ways then, and I knew that although it hurt like hell, it was for the best. What she said was true; I didn't know how to be happy, and if we stayed together, I knew my depression would rob her of her happiness too.

When I arrived home from the psychic reading, I went downstairs to my room to read the shamanic book. Despite my indifference with the world, the world of the supernatural still held interest for me. Five pages into the book, the message from Densel became clear.

On the page was the word "Acorns."

Densel must have given me the message as a confirmation of some sort. I scanned the different exercises in the book. A series of poses were prescribed, and they sometimes accompanied visualization techniques. I couldn't bring myself to believe that these techniques could attract more wealth or happiness into my life. It just didn't make sense. How could simple physical exercises and meditation change my life?

I can honestly say that there was no way I would have tried any of the exercises if it wasn't for Densel's message and its confirmation in the book. That was how my spiritual journey started.

Thank you, Densel. Wherever you are.

Fruition

I performed the exercises every night in the downstairs of my parents' house. I felt like an idiot, posing like various animals and then going directly into meditation, but the results came more quickly than I could have imagined.

My dreams became amazing and colorful. They contained animals, people, and situations that I didn't fully understand, and they were wonderful forms of entertainment if nothing else. My forced isolation from the world due to lack of employment and a relationship helped focus my energy on the exercises. It was only a few short months before my life started to turn around. New friendships were forged and I started to rebuild my old personal training business. In four months, not only had my depression totally left me, but I was making more money than I had in years and having a great time doing it.

Before I knew it, my ex girlfriend was also attracted back into my life. And that was when I cut back on my shamanic practices. Some part of me knew that getting back together with her was the wrong decision, but a large part of me missed her as well. I was torn, and I think she was too. So we decided to give our relationship another try.

I knew that the shamanic practices had attracted the success I was experiencing in my life. I never would have believed that my life could be good again, but it was. And like all people that experience success, I somehow forgot what had gotten me there in the first place. I continued some spiritual work, but the fact remained that although spiritual work could produce miraculous results, it most often pointed out the obvious misalignments in one's life. It was up to me to adjust my life according to the misalignments as I went.

Unfortunately, some corrections required pain.

My relationship with my girlfriend had become a close friendship. I knew she felt it too, because she would ask questions about the future, as if fishing for an answer that would confirm that she was in the right place in her life. One day she turned to me and said, "Do you want to be just friends?"

I wasn't ready to make the decision. I figured that there was something wrong with me, and that was the reason why we weren't able to connect properly. I was also aware of many other guys that complained of their relationships. And I thought it was possible that all relationships evolved into what I had with my girlfriend. A friendship.

The months rolled on, and my life started to dismantle again. My enthusiasm for my work left, my clients sensed it and one by one they faded away. I grew more dependent on playing hockey or spending long hours at the gym to power myself out of my dark mood. What made things worse, was that I had a shoulder injury caused from hockey that wasn't going away, and it was tearing away the little joy I received from playing sports and working out. Soon, it seemed that all pleasure had been squeezed from my life. I felt like a robot, just going through the motions, struggling to act like the happy people.

My twin brother, Jamie, watched this. And it seemed like the spiritual life beckoned to me once more.

Curiosity

Many pleasures had left me in life, and curiosity might have killed the cat, but I firmly believe that it kept me alive. My depression seemed to work like a fertile ground for the search for mysteries of the universe. Everything I knew bored me, but the unknown instilled a sense of excitement.

Jamie met me for lunch one day and said, "Jason, you have to see Arathi Ma."

"Arathi Ma?" I struggled to pronounce the name.

"She's an energetic healer, but she's psychic too."

I had numerous encounters with psychics, and although they might have been right about a few details in my life, I could never decipher which advice to listen to and which advice to ignore. My last visit gave me one jewel of information that started me on the spiritual path, so

I considered myself ahead of the game. I saw no reason to see a psychic again, unless the psychic could fix my problems as well as pinpoint them.

"No thanks," I said. "Psychics are always partially right, and I don't want to pay someone to tell me shit I already know."

Jamie leaned forward in his chair. "Arathi Ma is different. She doesn't just tell you stuff, she heals you too. She might be able to help with your shoulder."

My shoulder injury was quite extreme. I had dislocated it numerous times, and the only real solution to the problem was surgery. "How is she going to heal my shoulder? By wiggling her fingers above it, or something?"

Jamie shook his head. "Can you just trust me? Arathi Ma is different. If anyone could heal your shoulder with energy, she could. Besides, she can do a lot of other things. Above all I hope she can turn you from an asshole into a half-decent human being."

I laughed. Jamie had gotten me, lynched me with my curiosity. I decided to see Arathi Ma. Perhaps she would have the answer to my depression.

I made the forty-five minute drive to Arathi Ma's office in Vancouver. She worked out of a townhouse. I admit excitement. My brother was more of a scientific-minded sort of guy, and if he believed in Arathi Ma then I decided that there was something there worth investigating.

I parked in front of the townhouse and walked up to the glass door and knocked. A beautiful, middle-aged woman answered the door. She wore her medium length, silver hair up with a clip and she covered her slender body with a white, buttoned sweater with a dark gray turtleneck underneath. Completing the ensemble with dress pants, Arathi Ma appeared professional, almost as if she could double as a counselor or a life coach, hardly what I expected from an energetic healer.

She beckoned me inside and directed me to a room with several couches. A massage table covered with blankets sat off to the side. I sat down on one of the white leather couches and twiddled my thumbs. I wasn't sure what to expect, but due to Arathi Ma's professional nature, I couldn't help but feel nervous.

Arathi Ma sat across from me in a white leather chair that matched my own, and said, "How can I help you?"

"My brother says that you are really good at what you do." Although, I wasn't sure what that actually was.

"What brings you here?" She was direct and to the point.

It was a pretty general question, and I have to say that it was hard to answer. Curiosity was what brought me there. I wanted to see what she could do. I was also baffled by an overwhelming feeling of love I had towards this woman.

"My brother says that you can do stuff with energy. I guess I'd like to know what's possible."

She smiled. "You struggle with a busy mind, don't you?"

I didn't really know what that meant; I figured that all minds were busy. Wasn't that what minds were designed to do?

"I guess so," I said.

"Close your eyes," she said.

I did as I was told. I peeked once and saw that her eyes were also closed and her head was turning back and forth. I shut my eyes and waited.

A minute passed and then Arathi Ma spoke. "Now open your eyes." Her dark green eyes bored into me. "What do you notice?"

I glanced around me and noticed that everything seemed brighter. Actually, it seemed like someone had turned up the dimmer switch in my head. The world had seemed like a dark and gray place to me for as long as I could remember, and now it seemed like color had entered it once more. "Brighter." I smiled. "It's like someone's turned on the lights. Things seem crisper as well, almost like I'm wearing my glasses."

Arathi Ma smiled. "Good. The world appears different when you're in your core. The filters of the mind block out real experience. Do you understand?"

"Not really." I had no idea what the hell she was talking about.

"Don't worry about it. Your soul knows, and it hears everything I'm saying." She then motioned me to the massage table in front of a huge bay window. She left the blinds part way open so that the daylight from the cloudy sky could stream in.

I lay on the table face up, and Arathi Ma covered me with a blanket. I inhaled deeply and smelled incense and flowers. Arathi Ma then held her hands a foot above my chest and proceeded to scan my body from head to foot. "Close your eyes and relax," she said.

I lay on the table for about ten minutes before I heard Arathi Ma speak. "I see all of these dogs around you. What is that about?"

"I don't know, but I've been dreaming of dogs every night for about a year."

Her hand hovered above the left side of my abdomen. "There is a blockage in your spleen. Tell me, what happened just before your twelfth birthday. You're holding onto that trauma here." She pointed to where my spleen was located.

"My dog died." I still felt horrible about it. My brother and I had gone outside at night to ride our bikes. We lived on a street with very little traffic so I didn't worry when I let my dog off the leash so that she could run with us. As luck would have it, one car did speed down our deserted road that night.

Arathi Ma said, "How did your dog die?"

The coincidence wasn't lost on me. Arathi Ma detected a blockage in my spleen. "My dog was hit by a car. She died of a ruptured spleen."

I opened my eyes and found that Arathi Ma's gaze met mine. "It wasn't your fault."

I couldn't control myself. Grief came welling up from inside. I felt like a pussy crying over a dog that I had lost over twenty years earlier. No one knew how many nights I had grieved for the mistake I had made when I was only twelve years old. My dog, Flare had depended on me to keep her safe and I had failed.

Arathi Ma, seemingly sensing my thoughts, said, "It wasn't your fault. Do you know that?"

Of course I didn't know that. How could her death not be my fault? I had been too lazy to keep Flare on her leash.

I shook my head and I trembled with grief. Somehow I knew that one day Flare and I would meet again, and I'd have to explain to her how I was a spoiled, irresponsible kid that was too lazy to take proper care of her. I had decided long ago that a fiery death was too good a fate for me.

Arathi Ma held my gaze. "You know it wasn't your fault, right?"

She wouldn't let it go. I gave in and shook my head. "No."

"It was her time," Arathi Ma said. "That was the way she chose to go."

I wiped my face and my body relaxed. Maybe my dog's death wasn't *entirely* my fault. Arathi Ma continued to hold her hands above my body for another twenty minutes and I felt a soothing comfort move through me. In those moments, I felt like I was at one with her. I had never felt at one with another human being and I suddenly understood why I had always felt alone.

I was disappointed when Arathi Ma informed me that the session was over. I could have lain on that table forever, absorbing the energy from her hands. Somehow her energy reminded me of where I belonged. I felt nurtured underneath it in a way that I never had before.

I got up, albeit slowly, and paid Arathi Ma for the session. I noticed that I struggled with coordination and using my mental faculties because of the extremity of my relaxation. I booked another session with her for the following week. The experience had been truly magical indeed. I no longer felt depressed in any way at all. I felt great -- like the entire weight of the world had been lifted from my shoulders. In that moment, problems were a distant memory to me.

I smiled all the way home in the car and I sang aloud to the songs on the radio. Life was good. Who was I kidding?

Life was great.

A True Guru

The time for our next session came, and I found myself sitting across from Arathi Ma. She was devoid of the warmth that I had experienced in my first session with her.

"How are you feeling?" she said.

"Pretty good. The last session was great. I felt really relaxed after." I smiled, looking forward to another healing session.

It seemed that Arathi Ma had other ideas. "So how can I help you?"

The issue of abundance had been an ongoing problem in my life for many years, and I remembered what my brother had said, "She's psychic too." I thought then that maybe there was a chance that Arathi Ma could give me some guidance on how to bridge the gap between career and happiness.

"What am I supposed to do with my life?" I said. I knew that it was a general question, but if there was such a thing as destiny and soul purpose and all that, I decided that perhaps Arathi Ma could tap into the answer.

Arathi Ma held my gaze. "There's something off with your second chakra. Is there something you need to do that you're avoiding?"

I thought of my relationship. How my girlfriend and I enjoyed different things. I enjoyed sitting down to have a coffee, she thought sitting at a coffee shop was boring. She enjoyed working hard so that she could go on vacation; I enjoyed working little so that my life was a vacation. We were opposites in many ways, but because she was such a good person with high integrity, I couldn't bring myself to leave her. I decided that the relationship wasn't the problem, I was. If I changed myself, then all would be fine between us.

At the time, I couldn't see how staying with her could do more harm than leaving.

Arathi Ma seemed to read my thoughts. "How's your relationship?"

"We're good. Like best friends."

Arathi Ma nodded, and said, "Sometimes it's easier to correct the things in our life that contribute to our unhappiness than to use spiritual principles to transcend our situation."

I changed the subject. I glanced at the massage table, hoping that I'd receive another healing. "Can't we just do a healing?"

Arathi Ma tilted her head. "This is healing. So what is it that you think you need to correct in your life?"

I knew that boredom had set into my relationship for me and my girlfriend, but I knew the pain that would be caused if we broke up again. I was torn. It seemed that no matter which direction I turned, pain waited for me. "I can't leave my girlfriend. She's not the problem. I am."

Arathi Ma nodded. "So you're not happy in your relationship?"

"I'm as happy as anyone else is, I guess," I said.

Arathi Ma wasn't buying it, and she sure wasn't appreciating the fact that I was lying to her. "Do you think she's happy in the relationship?"

I shook my head, remembering how many conversations we had about how difficult I was to be with, and how I wasn't good at expressing love for her.

"No, she's not happy. That's why I'm here. If I change, then maybe she'll be happy."

Arathi Ma's expression turned to one of sympathy. "Some people are not energetically in tune or right for each other. That does not mean that either one of them is flawed or wrong in any way."

The session came to an end, and I felt sorrow. The session had not given me what I wanted. It had only drilled me about the truths in my life that I wanted to ignore. Arathi Ma was unique in a way that I had never experienced before and I wanted to receive more of her magical healing abilities, but she gave me a different version of healing than I had wanted to receive that day.

It caused pain in my heart, but I paid Arathi Ma and decided to never go back.

Initiation

A year passed, and I continued my intermittent spiritual work. I'd sometimes practice Chi Gong in the backyard or meditate late at night in my bedroom. My discipline was sporadic -- most often I meditated a few times a week. My depression worsened and my zest for life was all but gone. I trudged through one day to the next, waiting for my next hockey game to lighten my mood. I'm sure that my girlfriend suffered as much as I did during this time, and many times I thought to myself that she would have been better off without me. I was like a five-year-old brat at someone else's birthday party -- I couldn't help but pop everyone else's balloons.

I awoke late one morning to find Jamie standing in front of my bed. "How's it going?"

"F-ing great. Screw off," I said. I was tired all the time and I could never get enough sleep.

"I have something you should try," Jamie said. I felt something hit the bed by my feet.

I lifted my head from my pillow to see a book-shaped box. "What is it?"

"You've been doing some of the meditation stuff, so I thought you'd be interested in listening to this."

I dropped back onto the pillow. "Use it yourself."

Jamie picked up the box, and brought it closer. "I paid almost a hundred bucks for this. Just listen to it, okay."

I felt a little guilty that he had spent so much money. A part of me resisted spiritual stuff because I wasn't convinced that it was the answer to my depression. After all, I had done a series of meditations and practices and I was still depressed. How could this box contain anything different?

"How do you know it works?" I asked.

"Billions of people can't be crazy. After all, it doesn't look like you've got anything else going on." He made an exaggerated gesture of gazing around my dirty room.

I chuckled and threw a pillow at him.

Jamie ducked, and then said, "Listen to the CD's in the box. I think you'll like it. Use it as an experiment and see if it works."

He had me then. I didn't have to believe in anything. I only had to use the techniques, and then I'd be free to slander them as much as I wanted. My negative side liked that.

I listened to the CD's in my car on the way to work. Thomas Ashley-Farrand was a master at explaining the mysteries of the universe. He explained through various metaphors how everything was vibration and that the key to changing one's life was through using various mantra formulas. There were mantras for health, abundance, protection, full enlightenment, and so on.

I decided to use one of the mantras that he had prescribed for abundance:

Om Shreem Maha Lakshmi Yay Namaha.

I practiced it every day, all day. My mood lifted somewhat, although depression still came in abundance, but at least I had hope for a better way of being. I searched for signs of synchronicity in my daily activities and had some sense of purpose again.

As I practiced my mantras, in the back of my mind I thought of the blissful peace that I had once experienced in Arathi Ma's presence and I hoped to experience it again. My brother urged me revisit her, but I knew that seeing her, didn't mean that she would heal me in the way I wished. Perhaps she would ask if I had corrected what was out of alignment in my relationship. I wasn't done trying to heal it on my own yet, so I came up with an excuse of why I wasn't seeing her.

At the time Arathi Ma's office was an hour drive away from me. "She's too far away. I can't afford to cancel my clients and lose the money," I said. At the time, I was a personal trainer, so it was a legitimate excuse. My brother accepted it, and moved on and I was thankful for it.

My brother was a great man, but when he got an idea in his head, he was like a Pitbull with a chicken in its mouth. I have never heard of someone dying from being "argued to death" but if anyone was capable of it, he was. Come to think about it, he would probably say the same about me.

Well, life they say has a hint of irony. I continued my spiritual practice, praying for a miracle to take away the depression that overtook me with regularity. And one day, I received a phone call from my brother. Only three weeks had passed since starting my first mantra discipline.

Jamie said, "Arathi Ma is practicing one day a week here in town out of her student's house. Some of the older people can't make the drive so she came to make it easier for them. Isn't that great news? Now you can see her, too."

Great, I thought. I was being compared to the disabled. Not that there was anything wrong with the disabled, but I was clearly not disabled. I felt guilty for being catered to as if I was.

This was the sign I had been waiting for. I knew I could not avoid sessions with Arathi Ma anymore. Not only was my depression coming with increasing regularity, I would have my brother to contend with if I did not go to see her. I had prayed for a miracle, and here it was.

A New World

I was nervous about my first session with Arathi Ma. I hoped that she wouldn't force me into making any decisions that I wasn't willing to make, but I knew somehow that she held the secret to healing some part inside of me.

I drove my Honda Accord up to a white and blue house where Arathi Ma worked. A large thick tree stood in the middle of the yard, blessing the house with shade. I knocked on the front door and heard an English accent come in a lady's voice, "Come in." A long brown-haired middle-aged woman answered the door. She smiled. "I'm Joselyn. You're here for Arathi Ma, are you?"

I nodded.

"Just go up the stairs and wait on one of the couches in the living room, dear."

I went upstairs and took a seat. Large purple amethyst rocks sat around the fireplace and several orange salt lamps sat on top of several coffee tables.

A few minutes passed and then Arathi Ma emerged from the healing room. She greeted me with a smile and beckoned me inside. The room was lined with bookshelves filled with spiritual subjects such as Tarot Card Reading for Beginners and the I Ching. Figurines of various fantasy creatures such as dragons and fairies stood on each side of the shelf as if to guard the mystical library.

I sat in one of the chairs beside the massage table and Arathi Ma sat in front of me. "So," she said. "I'm surprised to see you, what brings you back?"

I understood a little more about the nature of spiritual work after listening to Thomas Ashley-Farrand's teachings, so I said, "I guess, I'm ready now."

Arathi Ma said, "Good." And that was it. She didn't bring up any of our last conversation, nor did she ask me anything about my relationship. It seemed like she had forgotten about the entire thing. I was relieved; I needed her help and she must have known it. She went easy on me and I was thankful for it.

Each session brought new experiences, both spiritual and physical. One day I would lie on the table and she would hold her hands above me, filling me with energy. Warmth and a dreamy comfort would suffuse my body, taking all my questions and cares away. At the end of the session, she would then tell me what she saw and what had needed the most healing during that session. Every session she would say something to me that confirmed that she spoke truth. A subtle comment like, "How is your relationship with so and so?" Or, "What's that white stuff in your shoulder?" She did not know it at the time, but my brother had employed a healing technique on my dislocating shoulder. It was called Prolotherapy, where he injected glucose and anesthetic into the joint so that the ligaments would heal. It was a very common practice for people who wanted to investigate a non-surgical option to healing partially torn ligaments and tendons. Of course the "white stuff" Arathi Ma had seen was the glucose, or natural glue. It was holding my shoulder in place while it healed.

My life at home started to get more exciting as well. One night, I remember lying alone in my bed. I had just finished one of my mantra disciplines and I waited for sleep to take me. That particular night, slumber eluded me. I had the nagging, eerie sensation that something was in my room and I felt as if someone was standing over my bed. My fear didn't come from a place of danger, but more of not knowing what the presence was. I could compare it to a stranger watching you from the window. If you knew it was one of your friends, it would almost be funny, but if a stranger watched you, then the entire situation changed to "creepy."

I tried to ignore it, and I tossed and turned for a while before I finally gave up and sat up to speak to whatever was in my room. The presence was so strong and real to me, although I had never had an experience like it before. I merely told the presence to leave if it wasn't there in my best interests. The technique seemed to work because after that I managed to get to sleep.

Later that night, something jolted me awake. I lifted my head and saw everything in my room was normal…except for the native Indian guy floating in the middle of it. His eyes were frog-like in the way they sagged and a beautiful, longhaired, Native Indian girl was in his arms. The man was shirtless, wearing leather pants, and had a leather satchel strapped over his shoulder. He did not smile at me, but I sensed kindness in him. The girl on the other hand, grinned from ear to ear.

It was then that I realized that my eyes were closed -- a distinction tough to make at the time because even though my eyes were shut, my room looked exactly the same as if my eyes were open.

I could not wait to ask Arathi Ma what had just happened.

Two days later, my appointment with Arathi Ma came. Our session continued as normal, she would ask what I wished to work on that day, whether it was a physical injury or emotional state, and then I would lie on the table and wait for the miracle to happen.

The question burned in my mind the entire time. Most of my sessions started like this. I had questions, many questions, and slowly but surely as Arathi Ma worked on me, they would all blip out of my memory. I'd leave the session all blissful and happy, but later the questions would reemerge and piss me off to no end. How could I keep forgetting them?

I decided this time was going to be different. I clung to my question with every ounce of my will and quivered with the excitement of it. I knew that Arathi Ma could answer it. As the session progressed, a sneaky smidgen of doubt crept into my mind. I started to second-guess my experiences. Perhaps I had been tricked, or even tricked myself into believing that what I had seen was real. I changed my question from, "Who was the man and woman in my room?" to "What was in my room?"

I smiled. If Arathi Ma really knew everything, then this question would not be so hard for her to answer.

At the end of the session I got up off the table. "I have to ask you something?"

Arathi Ma smiled. She was accustomed to me forgetting my questions and stumbling over my thoughts after our sessions. "What is it?"

"What was in my room the other night?"

She frowned ever so slightly at the ambiguity of my question. "Still testing me, are you?"

I felt guilty. Since seeing, Arathi Ma over the last several weeks, her healings had made a significant shift in my mood. I was happier than ever. It seemed disrespectful to test her when she had already proven her worth, but I just couldn't stop myself. It was the curse of my curiosity coming back to haunt me.

I quickly thought of an explanation for my personality flaw. "I have to know if what I'm seeing is real. It isn't as much about whether your knowledge is real, but whether I'm really seeing something or if I'm somehow going crazy."

She nodded, and then closed her eyes. Her eyes twitched and she turned her head back and forth as if she was scanning some invisible document. "He was your brother from a previous life. He has no shirt on and a satchel strung across one shoulder." She hesitated. "He's with your sister. He wants you to know that he loves you very much. He's with you on your journey."

My eyes watered. She had described the Native man perfectly, and she even knew about the woman that he was with. Arathi Ma really knew things. She didn't flounder around with a bunch of guesses until something landed close to the mark. I guessed that the chance of her getting my vision correct was about one in a million.

She had confirmed that my experience was real and because of it all of my questions suddenly meant nothing. Gratitude flowed through me, knowing that someone watched over me, cared about me when I knew I wasn't worth caring about. My Native brother, as Arathi Ma had called him, watched over me. He had seen my entire life, every good and bad thing I had ever done, and yet he still remained by my side.

Comfort flowed through me from my head to my toe. My invisible brother had reached out to me in my time of need and gave me something I very much needed: love.

Grounding

Each session with Arathi Ma was different than the previous. Our next appointment was on Friday morning. I personally trained a client at seven and another at eight thirty. I had never been much of a morning person, so my usual routine was to take a nap after training my morning clients. Of course, when the day came for my next appointment with Arathi Ma, taking a nap was impossible. I lay in my bed and stared at the ceiling. The anticipation of another session was too exciting for me, despite how tired I was. I tossed, turned, and finally gave up on the nap idea altogether and went early to my appointment early instead.

I waited in the living room on the couch in eager anticipation of my healing session. I practiced my mantras while I waited and I wasn't waiting long before I noticed several golden sparks appear in the air. I rubbed my eyes, gazed at the wall again, and noticed that every ten seconds another spark would appear. I also noticed a high-pitched sound in my ears that I didn't hear anywhere else but in the presence of Arathi Ma.

Many books on spiritual masters that I had read had highlighted such phenomena and it was common for students to merely sit in the presence of a master rather than listen to teachings or ask for guidance. It was said that the energy alone transmitted all the information needed. After that realization, I made a mental note of showing up early for every visit so that I could absorb more of her energy. I thought of it as the Costco of healing, or receiving healing in bulk.

The time for my session came and Arathi Ma gestured me into the healing room. It was sunny outside and Arathi Ma left the window open to allow the sound of rustling trees to enter the room. The cawing of crows from a nearby tree served as ambience while a gentle, temperate breeze suffused the room.

I sat in the chair across for her. "So how are you?" She tilted her head and bored into me with her dark, green eyes.

"Good," I said, knowing that it was only a half-truth. My depression was a demon that did not want to die. It would disappear for several days to reemerge a day later with greater enthusiasm. Her healings had at least given me some respite from the darkness of the depression, but it was clear that our work was not yet finished.

Arathi Ma stared at me, as if she was reading my thoughts. She repeated her question. "How are you?"

I have to say that I must have had balls of iron. I knew that this woman could read thoughts, but still my pride prevented me from telling her the truth about how I felt.

"Good," I repeated.

She tilted her head at my answer – she didn't believe a word of it. Instead of a direct confrontation however, she merely said, "How are you sleeping?"

I slept a lot, but it wasn't a restful sleep. More like the tossing and turning dream-filled type of sleep. I was usually more tired after sleeping than when I went to bed and I started to wonder if I was a werewolf. The state of my pillows and bed sheets were sure proof of it. It was rare for me to wake up with more than one pillow on the bed, and I twisted so much that I nearly choked myself to death with my blankets. Of course at the time, I thought that was how everyone slept, so when I answered, I at least *thought* I was telling the truth.

"Good. I sleep a lot." I smiled, embarrassed about how much sleep I needed. Most often even ten hours didn't feel like enough.

Arathi Ma nodded. "You're tired often, aren't you?"

"Isn't everyone?" I said.

"Yes, but when you go to sleep, you don't feel like you go away, do you? You are almost awake, but not. Let me ask you another question? Are you ever not tired?"

Arathi Ma was an expert at specificity in questions. She made me think of answers that I never knew I had.

I thought for a moment. Could I ever remember a time when I wasn't tired? No. Not unless I was exercising or in full adrenaline mode. That was the only medicine for my fatigue – an all out fight, competition, or extreme pain. Only those distractions could take me out of lethargy.

I answered. "No. I'm always tired." I felt the need to apologize. "I don't know why. There must be something wrong with me. I'm lazy or something."

I had been hearing that most of my life from people around me. "You're lazy. Why are you always tired? There's something wrong with you."

I cringed under the expectation of judgment from Arathi Ma.

She tilted her head, and gave me what I could only describe as the warmest, most compassionate expression I had ever seen. I wasn't a religious person and I didn't know a lot about Christian saints and prophets, but for some reason her expression reminded me of Mother Mary. I suddenly understood why Mother Mary was such a great woman. That this amazing love and compassion must have been in her eyes as well when she looked upon the suffering of others.

Arathi Ma said, "You're not lazy. Your energy just needs adjusting." She smiled while I hopped onto the massage table for the healing session. I was thankful for the distraction because it enabled me to hide my watering eyes.

One thing I've learned from the spiritual path was that no one was harder on you than yourself. I guarantee that every frustration you have with another human being; they have an even greater degree of that same frustration with themselves.

I closed my eyes while Arathi Ma scanned my aura. She accomplished this by holding her hands a foot away from my body. She scanned me from head to foot, and then moved her hands back to the points where she'd sensed an energetic block or problem. Sometimes the problems would also show up as entities, crystallized thought patterns, or attachments.

She held my feet and then said, "You need to ground more."

I didn't really know what that meant, although I was familiar with the idea. "Okay, good. No problem…how do I do that?"

Arathi Ma was already onto the next moment. "You didn't fully come here, did you?"

I didn't have an answer for that, so I just said, "What?"

"Your mother didn't expect you, did she?"

That was true. I was born an identical twin, but because my heartbeat was directly behind my brother's, the doctors with nineteen seventy-three technology did not sense that there were two of us. I can imagine my mother's surprise – or swear words –when I came into the world.

"No. The doctors told her to go on a diet because she was gaining too much weight. They thought that she was only going to have one baby, but surprise. Here I am. I was born thirty minutes after my brother, Jamie."

Arathi Ma closed her eyes, her head scanning back and forth. "Your mother and you did not have a contract so that you could fully be here. Answer me. Do you wish to fully be here?"

I thought for a moment. I didn't know that such a thing could be up for debate. I answered dumbly, "Yes."

Arathi Ma continued to scan, and then stopped. There was a release of some sort of energy, and I suddenly felt heavier on the table; almost like gravity increased fifteen or twenty percent. Relaxation moved through me, but I also felt more alive and awake at the same time. I almost laughed out loud, but suppressed my giddiness to a smile.

Arathi Ma closed her eyes again. "There's something in your DNA that needs activating" – her eyes fluttered – "the strand that's responsible for energy production. I'm going to activate that – with your permission of course."

I nodded; of course I wanted more energy. Who didn't?

"Activate it. Please," I said, images of what I'd do with the energy, flashing before my eyes. I have to admit, not all of my energetic aspirations were altruistic. While some might have visualized saving the world poverty situation, I imagined a stronger bench press, or lightning quick speed on the ice when I played hockey.

Minutes passed and then I felt a pulse of warmth move through my body. I remember now that up until that moment, I always had a certain paleness to my complexion. Ever since the day of the activation, the paleness left. I've been redder ever since, as if the floodgates of blood had been opened to my skin.

"Okay, we're finished. How do you feel?"

I felt great, but that did not explain what I felt when I got up. I placed my feet on the ground and stood up. The strangest sensation overwhelmed me. My legs suddenly felt like they were inside two big rubber boots. Like I had been placed into my legs for the first time in my life. They say you don't know what your missing if you've never had it. Well, I can honestly say that I have never been in my legs up until that point. It was like my soul had been pulled deeper into my physical body.

I walked around with a dumb smile on my face.

Arathi Ma smiled as well, as if she sensed what I was experiencing.

"This is weird, but so comfortable at the same time." I felt like there was hope for me yet. Perhaps I wasn't so flawed after all. I merely needed some energetic correction.

Arathi Ma sent me on my way, the echoes of her laughter on my mind as I drove home. I felt on top of the world. Like nothing could go wrong. I didn't realize what that feeling meant until I went to play hockey that night.

I felt great for the rest of the day. Night came and the energy continued, almost as if someone had supercharged me with a bolt of lightning. I had a men's league hockey game scheduled that night, and I was excited to see how the healing translated into physical performance.

The time came for the hockey game and I jumped on the ice for the warm up. This translated into practicing the movement of skating and puck handling, while moving in a large circle on one end of the ice. Giddiness doesn't properly describe my mood at the time, but it is the closest word I can come up with. Every stride I took felt full of energy and vigor.

When the game started, I was a whirlwind, chasing the puck down with ease, fatigue being more elusive to my legs than it had ever been. If memory serves me correct, in my first few shifts, I already scored two goals. To put this in proper perspective it was important to know what kind of player I was on this particular team. This team was filled with experienced hockey players -- more than a few of them had competed at the highest amateur level in their youth. I on the other hand, had only started playing hockey a few years earlier. I got by on speed alone, not skill. It was usual for me to score a goal in two or three games, not several in one game.

For my third goal, the puck took a fluky bounce, crawled along the ice at a snail's pace, and slid between the goalie's legs into the net. This caused me to laugh because I'm sure that there were many three year olds that could have shot the puck harder than I did. It was almost like the goalie was hypnotized into letting the puck into the net.

After I scored the third goal, my entire team knew that something wasn't right, although they couldn't properly understand what it was. Their lack of celebration was proof of it. Most often when a teammate scored a goal, he was greeted by his fellow teammates with a tap on the pads, or a "nice one". When *I* returned the bench, I was met with laughter and the shaking of heads.

One guy even turned to me and said, "How the hell did that go in, Gallant? You pay the goalie or something?"

The game continued, and so did the circus act. My energy continued also, and once again the puck was on my stick. I decided to test if my eyes were deceiving me, and I took my next shot from an impossible position, from center ice. The likelihood of scoring with such a shot was about one in a thousand. Well, as luck would have it, the goalie wasn't paying attention and, just as the puck was almost at the net, he skated out of it to allow the puck to pass by. The loud clanking sound jolted the goalie out of his daydream, and he seemed just as surprised as everyone else to find that someone had scored on him.

His shoddy goaltending was met with the wild swearing of his teammates. "Wake up, man. What are you? Drunk?"

Men's league hockey wasn't important in the big scheme of things, but to these guys, it was. I skated back the bench, my head so big with pride that my helmet was about to burst off of my head. I was surprised to find out that my team almost booed me. There was a lot of pride in who held the goal-scoring position on the team, and I was clearly not the first choice for it. I'm sure that it was humiliating for a star player to be outscored by a novice player such as myself.

I'll treasure that game forever because it confirmed to me that there were forces at work around me. Not only had those forces affected my own energy level, but they also had affected the actions of the goaltender. I wondered what else could this spiritual stuff do?

The Ripple Effect

Arathi Ma taught me that when a spiritual seeker starts their journey towards realization, that they not only affect their own life, but the lives of others around them. I guess I should have figured that out on my own because every time I silently repeated mantras in the same room as my girlfriend, she would say, "I don't know what it is, but you're irritating the hell out of me."

I guess that was why Arathi Ma never said anything about people around me "liking" the fact that I was doing spiritual work.

As the months passed with my sessions with Arathi Ma, and my daily practice of mantras and meditation continued, I noticed that my father was growing increasingly stressed at work. He was a policeman in the Forensics division. He witnessed human cruelty that no one should ever have to see. I did not see it firsthand, of course, but when you know your father had been working all night to collect evidence from a murder, and the next day the front page of the paper's headline listed a recent brutal event, you learned to put two and two together.

My father worked long hours. Most often, he left at three thirty in the morning – "Have to beat rush hour traffic" he'd say – and he'd return at four pm that afternoon, barring that no emergencies called him out. Now these hours might not seem extreme to some, but at least one night a week my father's pager would go off and he'd be collecting evidence from a crime scene until it was time for him to go back to work the next day. I cannot count the nights that he went with as little as two hours sleep.

Over the years his workload and responsibilities grew, and the backlogged court system put an increasing demand on him to organize more and more evidence. I cannot imagine the pressure he must have felt. One piece of information presented in the wrong way could destroy and entire case and ruin any chance of justice for the victims involved. Not that my father cared about whether justice was served or not. He cared most about the victims and their families. He drove himself to exhaustion trying to bring what little closure could come from convicting those responsible for the crimes.

I continued my spiritual practice and the odd time, my father would notice what I was doing. It was impossible to keep my practice secret of course because I was renting the basement from my parents at the time. Was I embarrassed about that? Yes. But as Arathi Ma would say, "All things are perfect the way they are."

It came time for my Friday session and I expressed concern over my father's stress level. Not only had he gone with a decreasing amount of sleep, he had experienced short black outs while he drove to work. Dizzy spells were a common occurrence for him, and these were only the symptoms that I knew about. I'm sure that my father's pride kept him from sharing any of his other symptoms with me.

Arathi Ma listened to my concern. "Would he be open to trying a session with me?"

"No, I don't think so," I said.

Although my father was the kindest person I had ever known, he could exhibit a stubborn streak from time to time. Who was I kidding? This man didn't know the phrase, "give up." I think the entire zombie concept came from him. He was the only man I knew who could find a way to walk even if both of his legs were hacked off. Come to think of it, if my father thought his feet were slowing him down, I could see him chewing them off and grinning about not having to waste time tying his shoes.

My father was a competitive weightlifter in his youth, and when his training did not make him strong enough, he decided to start a running routine on top of his three-hour a day weight training cycle. Well, after a short period of time, my father wasn't satisfied with the result. So instead of merely running, he decided to wear a backpack filled with weights. Shortly thereafter he complained of knee pain, but continued the training anyway. There were more examples of his willpower, but then again, I don't think I'd have enough room in this book to list them. I'm forever thankful for the willpower he passed on to me. The only trick was learning when to turn it off.

The fact of the matter was that my father would not want to admit weakness in any way, and in order to get him to see Arathi Ma, he'd have to admit – at least partially – that there was something wrong with him. My fear for his health outweighed the futility of my goal of getting him to see Arathi Ma. I decided that I'd have to set my will against my father's. A losing battle on the best day, but because he loved me so much, I knew that perhaps he'd indulge me a little.

Arathi Ma said, "You don't think your father would consider a healing with me?"

"No, but I'll convince him anyway." I didn't want to force something onto my father, but I decided life was better with him in it than out of it. And at the rate he was going, it wouldn't be long until he passed on into the after life. He was getting closer to retirement and it was a common occurrence for policemen to die within two years of leaving the force. If I had anything to do with it, he wasn't going to be buried with the countless other burned-out cops.

I called my father after the session and convinced him – through a series of guilt tactics and scientific reasoning – to do a healing with Arathi Ma.

He showed up that afternoon for his session and I waited anxiously at home for his return. Finally, from my room, I heard the front door to the house creak open. The sound of an opening coat closet followed and then the sound of discarded shoes hitting the foyer tile floor.

I rushed upstairs, anxious to hear how my father's session had gone. To my surprise, as my feet made their way up the steps to the second floor, my father's feet were making steps of their own to the third.

The Retreat Tactic.

My father was notorious for it. Anyone that knew him, complained about it. Anyone that sought a conversation with him, soon found themselves having a conversation with themselves.

I called it the Retreat Tactic.

My father was known for enjoying his alone time and he had devised several tactics in order to get more of it. I guessed that the heavy stress load at work required him to shut down and doing so in the middle of a busy conversation was impossible. When he didn't want to talk, he'd first employ the Retreat Tactic. If he was confronted by more than one eager conversationalist, he employed another strategy altogether:

The Question, Confuse and Scatter Tactic.

Many times my brother, mother, and I would be engaged in a conversation in the living room. My father – sensing that we would pressure him to join the conversation – would come into the discussion like a ninja. He'd dance a few steps into the living room, throw several sentences at us like ninja throwing stars, and then escape to the confines of the basement where he enjoyed a steady supply of television, radio, and books -- most often simultaneously. Any replies to his comments would be directed to his back, as he was already making his way out the conversation as fast he came into it. My mother, brother and I would be left shaking our heads at each other.

"There he goes to the cave again," Mom would say.

Well, seeing as I was being exposed to the Retreat Tactic, I decided to come up with a tactic of my own.

The Annoy The Hell Out Of My Dad Until He Told Me What Happened Tactic.

I heard the door to my father's room close like the drawbridge to King Arthur's kingdom. Dad wasn't tired, he just heard me making my way up the stairs and didn't want to talk to me. I knocked on the door to his room.

"What?" came the reply.

"What do you mean 'what'? How'd it go? What did she tell you?"

"She's a witch," Dad said.

I sighed. "She's not a witch, Dad."

"Yes she is."

Dad hadn't been to church for years, but all of sudden he was getting real Catholic on me.

"What happened, Dad?" I repeated.

"She knows stuff. Kind of reminds me of Mother Mary." There was silence, as Dad collected his thoughts. "She's still a witch, though."

"Quit avoiding the question. How'd the session go?"

I heard the movement of blankets and creak of a bed. "Said I was fine. Just too much stress, that's all."

I waited for more details. It was quickly apparent that he wasn't going to share them with me.

I tried to spark more conversation. "So…you're fine."

"Yup. All good. No problems. Just tired. Gonna nap now. Talk to you in bit."

Apparently, I had been dismissed from a superior officer. I admit that I saluted him through the door, but it wasn't the kind of salute that got someone promoted.

My father was being his old stubborn-ass self again. "All good." How could he be all good? My father had been complaining of heartburn for ten years, sleeplessness for five, and the odd dizzy spell or black out for the last few months. How could he just be fine?

In all the sessions I had with Arathi Ma, none of them could have been described in one or two words. Even if someone was fine, she'd have a detailed report of how they were fine, what was happening around them to maintain their fineness, and what to continue to do in order to increase their fineness.

Dad was holding back and I knew it.

I immediately emailed Arathi Ma, telling her about my growing concern for my father's health. I told her the symptoms that he had exhibited and what he had told me about their session. I told her that I knew the importance of discretion and that I wasn't asking for the intimate details revealed in the session with my father. I only wanted to know if my father's health was in serious jeopardy, and if there was something his family should be doing about it.

Arathi Ma's email was quick, as if she had been waiting for me to contact her. She sent me a lengthy email. She was quick to point out that she could not share the intimate details of the session, but she was concerned for my father. She said that he needed to take three months bed rest. Immediately! She suggested a number of scenarios that would unfold if he didn't do it, and a number of things that had happened already that not even Dad was aware of.

I had realized my father was sick, but I didn't realize *how* sick. She also said that it was possible that he had already experienced a mini-stroke. Something that he could recover from, but not something to be ignored.

I spoke to my mother about my dad's situation and she acknowledged that something had to be done. She was also familiar with Dad's stubbornness and knew that he wouldn't just take time off work. His famous mantra was, "I got no time." His workload would not allow him to take time off. If he did, he'd only return to from vacation to a workload twice as large as when he left. There was no one to replace him and no one else to depend on. He was truly chained to his position.

We came to a stalemate and in the end my mother agreed to speak to him. She'd ask him to take time off work, although she already knew what his answer was going to be.

I also knew the futility of the situation, and decided that maybe – for now – I was powerless to affect change. My father was grown man, and if he didn't want to take care of himself, I couldn't make him…yet.

Well, it seemed, the universe had other ideas.

I went to bed that night, troubled at my helplessness in the situation. I called my girlfriend, had a brief conversation about it, and then went to bed.

Three-thirty a.m. my phone rang. I jolted awake with such a start that I nearly fell out of my bed.

"Hello," I said.

There was crying on the other end of the phone. It was my girlfriend. "Jason, it was so bad."

"What happened? What's going on?" A million scenarios flashed through my mind.

She sobbed. "I had a bad dream. This has never happened before."

"It's okay. I've had lots of bad dreams. Everyone does. It's just a dream." I tried to console her as best as I could, but like many guys I was horrible at it.

"No," she said. "This wasn't a normal bad dream." Her words were hard to make out through her crying. She was really shaken up. We had been together for several years and I had never seen her like this.

"Tell me about it."

"I was in the middle of a normal dream and then suddenly this sound came into it. I started having some sort of seizure and then I saw the palm of a hand. One of those old black and white films with those numbers counting down before the movie starts was on it. My head started to hurt so bad, but I had to watch the movie. After the numbers counted down, your dad appeared. He was wearing that old blue, Bum Equipment sweater. He walked into the kitchen of your house, and then he fell down. And"—

More crying interrupted her words. Her sobbing continued for a moment as she gathered the strength to answer. "And he died. It was so sad. Your father died."

I felt like I had been punched in the gut.

I know that some of you who are reading this story will say that it was only a dream. It wasn't. I knew my girlfriend too well to toss away her intuition on a whim. She was a very controlled rational human being. She did not believe in psychics or in supernatural phenomena. She didn't condemn any of it either, but the new age world just didn't interest her in the slightest. And even though something happened to her that she didn't understand or even believe in, she wasn't one of those people that discarded an experience on the premise that she didn't believe in it. She was a part of my life, and it was clear that my spiritual disciplines were affecting her.

Her sobbing dwindled as she finished her description of the dream. She even laughed a little at the ludicrousness of it affecting her so strongly. "I feel better now. Silly, too."

"You're not silly," I said. "You must have tapped into something."

"Well, I don't want it to happen again; my head hurts," she said. The sound of teeth chattering came through the phone. "My ear hurts too and my jaw feels so tight. I hope I didn't have a seizure or something."

I was aware that she had experienced some sort of spiritual purge. I felt guilty about my spiritual disciplines affecting her so strongly. It was clear that her body wasn't ready to receive such a powerful burst of energy

I thanked her for sharing the dream with me. Her experience gave me a renewed sense of conviction in helping my father. I knew that the message in her dream had been intended for me. If I didn't do something, he *was* going to die.

The next day, I sat down with my mother and told her about my girlfriend's dream, Arathi Ma's visit with my dad, and the many reasons why the information of both of them should be trusted.

Mom nodded in agreement. "But what can we do about it?"

"We do the only thing we can do. We call his boss," I said.

My mother had expressed the strategy in the past, but had cast the whole idea aside because she knew how angry and embarrassed my father would be about it.

She sighed. "You're sure. Your dad will be so mad." That was the first time I had ever seen my mom worried about angering my father. My entire life I had seen my mom sway him to her way of seeing things, without much of an argument. I guess my mother's true wisdom wasn't in using willpower, but in knowing which battle was worth winning and which one wasn't.

"Don't worry, Mom. We'll call his boss, and if you think Dad will be too angry, you can tell him it was all my idea." A scenario of my dad using his standard issue nine-millimeter to dispose of my kneecaps flitted through my mind, but I quickly pushed it aside. My girlfriend had suffered too much from her dream for me to ignore it. I wasn't about to let her sacrifice go to waste.

My mother nodded. "No, if we're going to do this, we're in it together." She thought for a moment. "Do you think it would okay if we didn't tell him it was us? At least for now."

I nodded and suddenly felt like we were two siblings discussing a secret that we wanted to keep from our parents.

My mother then made the call that ended my father's career as a policeman -- the most honorable, dedicated man the police force had ever seen.

Damn, I felt guilty about that, but it was the only choice we had. My priority was always my father's happiness and wellbeing. I knew that eventually he'd see it, too.

My mother hung up the phone and I could see the same guilt mirrored in her expression. "Jesus, I hope this is the right thing. I feel so bad. The Force is his life."

"Yes," I said. "And if he stays longer, it'll be his death. Do you want him to feel important or do you want him alive?"

She nodded. "I know. I still feel like hell about it."

A few hours later I received a call from my girlfriend. Due to the sleeplessness of her night, she had gone home after nursing school to take a nap.

"It happened again," she said. "But this time it wasn't as bad. I had a little bit of the seizure thing, and I saw the film projection on the hand."

"What did the film show?"

"It was confusing. It only showed stairs. The stairs led upward. What do you think that means?"

I had a book on interpreting dreams in my room downstairs. I ran down to grab it and flipped through the pages. To my surprise there was a passage on dreaming about stairs.

It said, "If one dreams about stairs, and they lead upwards, it means that all is good."

I told my girlfriend about what the upward stairs meant and thanked her profusely. Her dream had guided me, and then confirmed that I had taken the right action in accordance with the message. Her confirmation also helped lift some of the guilt my mother and I experienced. I was also aware of Arathi Ma's presence during the entire process and she also had my eternal gratitude for being the catalyst in saving my father's life.

My mother and I waited anxiously for my father's return from work. The front door swung open with a creak and we heard a briefcase drop onto the floor. In a moment, he wandered into the living room. His stride was devoid of its usual purpose; his glance scanned the living room without landing its attention on anything in particular. The room became a steam bath of my mother's guilt and my father's hopelessness.

My mother played dumb. "What is it, Jim?"

My father's expression didn't change; I'd never seen his eyes so out of focus. "I think I got fired." He then turned and made a slow ascent of the stairs to his room.

My mother and I stared at each other, knowing the ramifications of what we had done. Not only had we succeeded in removing my father from work, we'd accomplished something else that we hadn't intended. We'd reinforced the idea of failure in my father. Even now, in the midst of his blackouts, stomach problems, and extreme stress, he was thinking that he had somehow failed. That he hadn't worked hard enough and that was why he had been told to stay home.

"Maybe we should tell him," I said.

My mother shook her head. "Not yet. He won't understand."

Enough bombs had dropped for one day, so I acceded to her wishes. In the end, we had pulled Dad from the fire. Now the healing could start.

My Dad returned from his room and walked into the adjoining kitchen. My heart almost stopped. He wore the old Bum Equipment sweater that my girlfriend had seen him wear in her dream.

It was the sweater that he had worn when he had died.

Another confirmation, I noted. When my guilt was running at its highest, the sign had come to show that my mother and I had done the right thing.

Bliss

Next Friday it came time for another session with Arathi Ma. I rushed to get to the house where she worked so that I could arrive early to watch the "Fireworks Display" in the living room. Not to be disappointed, sparks filled the air and I felt strangely energized in their midst. Orange salt lamps glowed in the corners of the room while a purple amethyst that Joselyn had named Harry sat to my left in front of a barren fireplace.

The entire room buzzed from Arathi Ma's presence and I could only describe it as a very high-pitched sound. When I gazed at the white walls in a way akin to staring at an abstract painting, random bright white sparks danced before my eyes.

It wasn't long before I learned that my back would ache if I stayed in the energy for too long. It was almost as if my body couldn't take too much of it and I could only compare the sensation of it to when

I drank too much coffee, except instead of drinking one or two pots of coffee, compare it to ingesting fifty. Inevitably, a tension headache would adjoin the backache. Several times I tried to sleep it off, but my wired state prevented me from falling asleep.

I had read that such sensations could have been attributed to the activity of the Kundalini energy, also known as the Cosmic Serpent in Shamanism. When the Kundalini was even partially activated in a person, they started to seek out their own divinity because that was when the Kundalini made its way up the spine so that it could return home into the Great Infinite. According to Thomas Ashley-Farrand, this path could take thousands of lifetimes.

I rubbed my neck; I couldn't imagine feeling wired for that long.

The door to the healing room swung open and a young, dark haired woman said her goodbyes to Arathi Ma and left. My heart started beating faster. I was so excited for my appointment, for the mystery of what I would experience today. I was so convinced of Arathi Ma's power that if some mystical creature suddenly burst through the wall during the session I wouldn't have been surprised.

Arathi Ma met me with a smile that warmed me from the inside out, and beckoned me into the room.

I shared what happened with my father, and gave her a summary of the past week's events. I also told her that I wished to be more abundant so that my father wouldn't worry about me so much. I knew that his stress with my instable finances would only increase now that he had been taken off work. He was still receiving his full wage, but I knew that he'd use his situation as an excuse to reinforce his idea that life was instable, dangerous, and just plain shit in general. If I had more money, then perhaps my father could have an easier time relaxing.

Arathi Ma nodded and smiled. "What mantras are you doing right now?"

"I listed a series of mantras. I mixed and matched them like a warlock in an old black and white horror film."

Arathi Ma gasped. "Those formulas are very powerful, you know. I'm not sure if mixing them is the best thing for you."

"What can I say? I love this stuff. It's the only thing that's ever made me happy," I said. "Besides, that's what I have you for, right? You'd tell me if something was going wrong." I probably gave her the dumbest smile she had ever seen.

Arathi Ma smiled, disarmed by my absolute faith in her. "Yes, but if I see something's not working, you have to listen to my advice."

"Of course," I said, nodding with enough enthusiasm to break my neck. I couldn't wait to get on with the session. My journey had produced such amazing results that my enthusiasm for the path had grown tremendously. And what made things worse was the fact that I had the uncanny capacity to excite myself to death; just sitting in that room with Arathi Ma was about enough to make me explode. I suddenly realized where all the rumors of the phenomena of instantaneous disintegration came from. I'd seen a show once where people just blew up into a mist with no apparent reason. Probably an urban myth at best, but if it wasn't, I was sure about to find out.

"Okay, so you are doing the Lakshmi mantra?"

I nodded. "A few hundred a day, sometimes more." It was the same mantra that had attracted Arathi Ma into my life.

"Well, if you are initiated into such a mantra, it becomes stronger for you. Did you know that?"

I hadn't realized that there was such a thing. "No."

"Would you like to be initiated?" Arathi Ma smirked with a knowing of what my answer would be, almost as if she was toying with my impatience.

Again her words were met with a nodding of such fierceness that my head almost fell off. She laughed, her eyes squinting with such joy and innocence that it made my heart hurt. I'd never seen someone laugh like her before. I was accustomed to the type of laughter that came from sarcasm, pain, and the ridicule of others. Hers had none of those things.

She sat in a chair before me, her right foot placed firmly on the floor while the other one was tucked under her. She gestured for me to sit with my palms up and eyes closed.

"Just receive," she said. She closed her eyes in meditation for a minute, and then she outstretched her hand to touch my forehead. She sang the mantra, "Om shreem maha Lakshmi yay namaha."

Again I grew relaxed while warmth flowed through me. It was very subtle, not overwhelming in any way, but the strangest thing happened. My eyes were closed, like Arathi Ma had instructed me to do, but I had the strangest sensation that she had four arms. It was almost as if I could *feel* them in front of me.

I expressed my experience to Arathi Ma.

"That is because Lakshmi has four arms. I become her when I give the energy to you."

Lakshmi is known as the goddess, or energy, of abundance. She is known as the mother, the nurturer, the one that gave you prosperity and happiness in all its forms. Happiness looked different for everyone, but whatever the ideal was, Lakshmi's energy was invoked to bring about that ideal. I found it ironic that I had chanted Lakshmi mantras to attract a woman that would initiate me into the Lakshmi energy.

The initiations didn't end there. The next week I should have known that something special was about to happen when the door to the house suddenly opened as I reached for the handle. No one was hiding behind it and no one had opened it for me. It just opened on its own, as if by my thoughts. I passed it off as the wind, but my observation was only partially right.

That day when the healing portion of my session ended, Arathi Ma said, "You're ready."

"For what?"

"To receive a higher vibration. You've done enough cleaning work on your energetic field. So now you're ready to receive it."

She said that it was okay for me to lie on the table to receive the transmission. She placed her right hand on my heart while she chanted a mantra. "Arut Perum Jothi. Arut Perum Jothi. Thanip Perung Karunai. Arut Perum Jothi."

The lightest fluffiest feeling I had ever had spread throughout my chest. Excitement for life suffused my entire being and all of sudden everything in the world looked good. I was used to Arathi Ma's pleasant energy, but this energy was different in a way that it was higher in pitch and filled me with far greater bliss.

I got up off the table with such enthusiasm coursing though me that if I opened my eyes any wider, they would have fallen out. A tinny music played softly in my ears and in that moment I understood why monks spent their entire lives in a monastery searching for God.

I kept saying to myself. "I didn't know. I didn't know."

In the moment of the initiation, the simple concerns of my life no longer mattered. In an instant, my priorities changed and I was suddenly free from all of my stresses. I was free from the constant stirrings of my mind and the most relaxing, ecstasy coursed through my heart and into every corner of my being.

My world changed in that moment. I walked around for two weeks in a blissful fog. Mentally I was clearer than I'd ever been, but I had also never been as relaxed and at peace with everything around me. I'd repeat mantra only a few times before the sensation of bliss and ecstasy grew stronger.

Arut Perum Jothi.

Arut Perum Jothi.

Thanip Perung Karunai.

Arut Perum Jothi.

No longer was spirituality a way to solve my problems. It became the search for the place where there *were* no problems.

Prophecy

Shortly after the initiation I received an email from Arathi Ma informing me of an upcoming weekend workshop. In this workshop she explained that she would give further initiations and teach different tools to work with on the spiritual path. I have to admit that I wasn't sure what to expect. Up until that point I had only worked with Arathi Ma in individual sessions and enjoyed them tremendously. The unknown always held the greatest fear, and I have to say that a workshop with a bunch of people that I didn't know was a little intimidating. I wasn't sure what to expect, although if Arathi Ma said it would be good for me, then I had to believe that it was true.

The weekend of the workshop came and I set out to Arathi Ma's Vancouver office with a Joselyn, the woman who owned the house where Arathi Ma worked in Maple Ridge, and my brother's girlfriend, Tara who had also been enjoying sessions with Arathi Ma for quite some time. We were told to wear white because it was better for the absorption of the energies introduced in the workshop. So off we went, looking like three marshmallows. An ironic thought, seeing as I had since learned that the name Arathi Ma translated into "Divine Fire." I wondered which one of us was going to get roasted.

Since I had last been to Arathi Ma's office, she had moved her healing space from her townhouse to a small office on the second floor of a building on Broadway. The room was about fifteen by fifteen feet, and had space enough for group meditations and healings. There were about twelve of us in all, and we all sat in a circle awaiting Arathi Ma's instructions.

She greeted us and handed out booklets outlining the various exercises that would be performed over the next two days.

The majority of the workshop centered on extra initiations of the "Arut Perum Jothi" mantra and a combination of dancing, breathing, and yogic techniques. The Arut Perum Jothi vibration would be placed into other critical energetic centers of the body and then we would perform the dancing exercises to speed up the rate of absorption and clearing of the crystallized mind patterns and negative energy in our bodies. It definitely brought me out of my comfort zone. Don't get me wrong. At being an idiot, I was a professional, but that was in my youth, and usually after a drink or two and a crowd of friends to watch the entertainment unfurl. This situation, on the other hand, was in a room full of spiritual women of all ages. They were all nice and open, but I had no wish to offend them or cause a disturbance of any kind. I wasn't sure what the boundaries of social etiquette dictated in a situation that called for a bunch of strangers to dance together under spiritual pretenses.

Arathi Ma instructed us in the first technique called Fire Breath. It encompassed rapid breathing in and out of the nose for five minutes before we switched our breathing to a longer and gentler form. Those of you that have trouble turning off your mind, Pranayama, or energetic breathing, is definitely for you. They say that breath and thought are one, and I agree. Since the learning of Pranayama, deeper and deeper meditations have been possible for me.

After the Pranayama, Arathi Ma turned on some music and guided us through a series of hand movements while we all danced in a circle. It wasn't long before I decided the whole guarded approach to the workshop was a waste of time. For example, one particular part of the dance was to place one hand on top of our head while we placed the other hand over top of one of the various energy centers in our abdominal area. We already looked ludicrous in our white outfits, dancing around like a bunch of drunken angels, but holding our hands on our heads like we were in a perpetual salute to each other was just weird.

In that moment I decided that it was okay for my internal idiot to come out. I invented a whole series of dances. It wasn't long before many of us weren't taking ourselves too seriously, and the exercises became an opportunity to finally loosen up. It was a relief. Many of the people at the workshop were probably sick to death of being a certain way, or constantly performing to the expectations of their day-to-day life. I know I was. Finally this was a place where we could be ourselves; where we could be in alignment with Truth, as Arathi Ma would say.

The dancing ended with chanting for several minutes before moving into a meditation. My mind had never been so silent.

That night I was exhausted. I had received a number of energetic transmissions and performed the yogic exercises twice. The next day we continued with more transmissions and the practices.

The weekend was a success for me. I had gained some more tools in search for happiness and I applied them readily. Monday morning after returning from work, I performed the exercises on my own. I was twenty minutes into the meditation portion of the exercise when I fell asleep, and it was then that I had the most powerful dream I had ever had.

In the dream Arathi Ma stood on the roof of a house. Her silver hair was long and it whipped wildly in the howling wind. I had the sense in the dream that she was leaving. Leaving me. The emotions were so strong in the dream. So untamed. Sadness overcame me with such intensity that I cried.

"No!" I yelled, hoping that Arathi Ma could hear me above the wild howl of the wind. She couldn't hear me though, and her face was turned upward as she started to float towards the sky. She rose higher and higher, and I collapsed to my knees begging God to bring her back to me.

In that moment I felt something grab me by the back of my pants and draw me upward. Some invisible force pulled me into the sky until I was beside Arathi Ma. We rocketed higher and higher until everything became light.

I jolted awake, my eyes full of tears. The dream had seemed so real, but what did it mean? I knew that Arathi Ma played a very important role in my life, but the emotional power of the dream suggested something much larger than I could have imagined.

Journey

One day my mother asked me if I would go on a trip with my father to help him relax. She mentioned that as long as he stayed home, there were too many reminders of the stresses of work to haunt him. She thought a change of scenery would be good for him.

Thirty years earlier, my parents had moved from their hometown of Stephenville, Newfoundland. Upon joining the RCMP, my father had hoped to be stationed close to his hometown, but it seemed his superiors had other ideas. They, of course, chose the next most sensible location for him to start his career – the other side of the country. There was little choice for him at the time, the economy was bad – especially in Newfoundland's struggling fishing industry -- and many people had been out of work for quite some time. Like so many others in Newfoundland, my parents were forced to leave everything they had ever known so they could find work. They found what they were looking for in Vancouver, but I know that part of their souls never left Stephenville.

My mother decided that a trip back to our native land would be best to bring Dad's health back around. She had also been following my exploration of the spiritual world, and discovered that there was an upcoming Chi Gong conference planned in Stephenville as well.

It seemed like destiny. I would learn some new techniques to add to my toolbox, and my father would learn them as well. I had read a few books on Chi Gong and had experienced some of the physical healing. effects of its practice. Perhaps it was the perfect thing to ease my father's stress level. I on the other hand, was excited to return to a place I had not been for seventeen years. All of my memories of Newfoundland were happy. The people were more open and had an entirely different set of priorities than the people of the west coast. I was excited to share my experiences with my relatives still living in Stephenville, and to practice my spiritual disciplines in the beautiful open spans of nature.

I had one session with Arathi Ma before I left. I shared my plans of attending the conference and asked where Chi Gong fit with the spiritual practices that I had learned from her.

She shrugged. "An octopus might have more than one arm, but each one leads to the center. While the immediate result is different, the end result is the same. Don't forget about your other practices. Do them every day and when you come back we'll see if you're ready for the next initiation."

With her blessing to investigate Chi Gong, I was soon on a flight to Newfoundland with my father. Destiny, it seemed, was calling and through some strange mix up with my mother's air miles, my father and I were upgraded to First Class. I had never flown First Class before and I admit that I was immediately spoiled. I lay back in my seat and drifted off, thoughts of Arathi Ma constantly on my mind. I became aware then that the thought of her never left me. Every mantra I spoke, every meditation I performed, she loamed in the background of my mind. She was the very personification of my spiritual ideal, my spiritual path. I also thought of what she had said before I had left – the dangling carrot of another initiation waited for me when I got back -- and set myself to a new level of fervor in maintaining my disciplines.

We arrived in St. John's airport and upon figuring out the details of renting a car and collecting our luggage we were off to find our motel. Upon stepping out of the airport doors the wind blasted us with its welcome. It was the end of April, and there was no hint of warmth, but still the wildness of it felt like heaven to me. Immediately memories of when I was only a few years old came rushing back to me: riding my little green bicycle through a potholed gravel road in the trailer park where we lived, throwing rocks into the waves of the Atlantic from a rocky shore with the scent of the ocean whipped through my hair, and visiting my grandparents for Sunday dinner.

I was home.

We were exhausted by the time we checked into the motel. Newfoundland had served as a home for more than a few American Military bases, and decades earlier our motel had served as a barracks. When my father and I lugged our bags across several weed strewn patches of grass that served as lawns and arrived to our room, we felt like we had journeyed fifty years back in time. The curtains were brown and plaid, and the walls were so hollow that if any tenant passed gas from the room beside us or above us it could be heard in the most resounding way.

I was exhausted, so it didn't take long before I made my way to my bed. It looked comfortable enough, in its nineteen seventies sort of way, and it gave a mighty squeak when I sat upon it. I struggled to push the thoughts out of my head of the thousands of ways the bed could have acquired such a nasty condition. Let's just say that I slept with my pants on.

Soon sleep overtook me and that was when the dream came.

The dream started with thunderous footsteps. The kind of footsteps that told you to hide or else something really bad was going to happen. I remember hiding under a bed, praying that whatever approached did not hear my panic-stricken gasps. The wind howled and the roof was torn from the motel to reveal a dark sky with clouds illuminated only by the light of a full moon. The footsteps came closer, but I realized then that they were not in the motel, but in the sky above the clouds.

The footsteps halted, and then the source of them was revealed. A large, black head wearing a Viking helmet poked out from behind a cloud. It stared at me, and I sensed such power that I knew that it was a creature beyond man or animal.

I jerked awake, fully expecting a Viking fighting-utensil in the face.

The next day we started our journey across the province. I shared my dream with my father and he laughed and said, "Vikings were here long before anyone else. I should take you for a hike up on Gros Morne National Park. From there we can go to the old Viking settlement in L'ans aux Meadows. Many of the Viking structures still stand there today."

The journey to Stephenville would take an entire day's drive, and it was clear to me that this trip was far from relaxing. I did the majority of the driving in our rented little Ford Ranger truck, but I was eager to get to our destination so that we could rest. The long hours in the truck together turned out to be a blessing. We talked for a long time, seeing as my father couldn't use his usual Retreat Tactic. Although I'm sure he thought of it a few times as I drilled him about belief systems and how to find happiness. His inability to escape was largely due to the eighty kilometer per hour speed limit; he knew from his many years working the Traffic Division in the police force that he had little chance of surviving a duck and roll maneuver if he jumped out of the truck.

When we finally arrived to Stephenville to stay at my cousin's house, excitement overtook me. It was like living in a dream to be back where I was born. Sitting in the Lazy Boy chair at my cousin Kathleen's house took me to a place of renewed relaxation. I closed my eyes for only a moment, and I was suddenly greeted by the image of a leaping wolf. The vision was so powerful that I couldn't ignore it. I could compare it to someone suddenly installing a short movie in my mind. I had experienced visions during meditation, but never when I closed my eyes for a mere moment. What was happening?

That was my first evidence that different landscapes offered different energies. Newfoundland was often referred to as "The Rock." Anyone that has tried to dig a hole in its terrain could tell you where the name came from. When I was kid my Grandpa had asked me to dig a hole for him. After that, the word "shovel" and the word "dig" sent shivers through me with the remembered vibrations of sticking the metal end of the shovel into the ground to strike one rock after another.

After many conversations with Kathleen about the upcoming workshop, night finally came, and I am pleased to say that I slept soundly *without* the visitations of old Viking spirits. I did, however, have the company of my cousin's three elusive flat-faced cats. I only remember the name of one of them: Beauty. She was the ever-elusive white cat. When I awakened the next morning, I got up to go to the kitchen and I could feel her eyes poking around from behind a door. It took me some time before I managed to get a good look at her and discovered that her name was either an attempt at sarcasm, or the aging process had not been kind to her... or several of her nine lives had been stolen from her. Her long hair stood out in irregular tufts, giving her some thickness to the scrawny body that lay underneath and when she stared at you, the ever-present fear that coursed through her was obvious by the size of her eyes. In a passing thought, I feared her eyes would pop out of her head and bounce to my feet.

The white streak that was known as Beauty, disappeared when my father entered the kitchen. He turned his attention to the kitchen table and saw another cat lying on top of it beside the fruit bowl.

This cat was of the gray, longhaired persuasion. It lay flat on its back, legs spread wide as could be, enjoying the sun on its tummy. This cat knew how to relax because if its legs spread apart any more I feared that it would split in half.

"Yuck," Dad said.

Dad loved animals, but peanut butter and fur toast was not his favorite idea of breakfast. There, of course, was no fur in his plate, but I knew that my father's excessive sensitivity to animals around food was extreme. According to him, if an animal was in the kitchen, it had no business being there unless it was cooked and on a plate. He scowled, and pushed his plate aside. It seemed that the cat had dominion over this area of the house and I was suddenly thankful that Dad didn't have access to his standard issue nine-millimeter handgun. I gave the gray cat a few affectionate pats and they were met with an enthusiastic purr. There was something about that gray cat that I loved. When it looked at me, it really felt like a real intelligence was in those eyes.

"Well, we better get a move on," Dad said, checking his watch. Apparently, vacation time was held to a strict schedule.

I gathered my things and then we were off to explore the town of Stephenville. That was the day my father took me to where my grandparents were buried. Grandma had passed away four years earlier around the same time I had begun my spiritual journey and my grandfather passed away two years behind her.

I stood looking at their graves. Sadness overwhelmed me in that moment. Memories of my early childhood and how my grandparents took care of me came flooding back to me. My grandmother always carried a smile although she was quiet most often. My grandfather was the opposite of her as he was a bear of man; drinking and fighting in his youth was an all too common occurrence.

Despite all of those things though, he was a man of honor.

Grandpa told me a story once of an altercation he had in his youth. One thing led to another and fists flew, and as was the case most often, my grandfather claimed victory. In the altercation, he had broken the man's jaw. My grandfather felt guilty for it though, for his pride getting the better of him. He knew that it was wrong to hurt someone for the sake of pride, and when he discovered that the man would have to miss work because of the injury, my grandfather gave the man – his former enemy – the money he needed to support his family.

My father left me alone with the graves so that I could say goodbye in private. The graveyard was placed on top of a hill so that the wind from the ocean whistled over it in wild gusts. Perhaps, the wind was the language of the Newfoundlanders buried there. I could not ignore the feeling that my grandparents were watching me. I'm sure that many others that visit the graves of their loved ones would agree that they too feel the eyes of the deceased upon them.

I prayed in that moment for a rapid recovery for my father.

The Conference

Every day leading up to the conference included a trip to the beach to perform the yogic exercises that Arathi Ma had taught to me. The wind coming off the Atlantic was so cold at times that I thought my nose would freeze off. Most often the beach was empty except for the company of seagulls drifting on the wind. Their free nature reminded me of Arathi Ma and I often wondered if she missed me as much as I missed her.

One particular day, after finishing my yogic exercises on the beach, memories of my grandparents came to me. One moment my mind was empty and then thoughts of them suddenly popped in. In my childhood, going to Newfoundland had always meant seeing my grandparents, so I admit that there was a void in my heart where they usually resided.

I smiled as a memory of how my brother and I used to tease Grandpa came flooding back to me.

In one particular instance, my brother yanked Grandpa's elastic suspenders causing them to snap against his back. Grandpa yelped, and then proceeded to chase us all over the house, all the while slapping his leather belt against his hand in the most threatening manner. We'd laugh, seeing Grandpa's smile hidden underneath the furrow of his brow. After the game was finished, Grandpa would retire to the couch, either to play his accordion or continue a conversation with one of the relatives. Jamie, however, was unable to resist the thrill of the suspender game. He'd wait until the perfect moment when Grandpa was distracted and then Jamie would attack. There'd be a yelp, then my brother's uncontrolled giggling, and the game would start all over again.

I had heard many stories about the stubbornness of my grandfather, the conflict, the drinking, the fighting, but he was none of those things to me. Grandpa was the suspender game.

Gratitude for how my grandparents had treated me sprang forth from my heart. I thanked them and prayed that they'd find happiness wherever they were.

After that, I hiked my way back to my cousin's house. As I walked up the hill, a strange sensation moved through me. I was wearing heavy fleece sweatpants at the time, but for reasons I could not say, they felt even more comfortable. Actually, comfortable does not completely describe what was happening. My pants were absolutely, totally, indescribably cozy. It was like the softest most snuggly substance known to man was wrapped around my legs.

From that day forth, the cozy sensation continued every day after completing my yogic exercises on the beach. It was as if the practice of the exercises had unblocked some sort of comfortable energy in my body. Whatever it was, I was thankful for it. I walked around for several weeks in a perpetual state of absolute comfort. I was reminded again, that if everyone could tap into that feeling all the time, then there'd be little reason for the addictions of the world such as drugs and alcohol. It seemed to me, that the entire body was already the highest drug experience; it just took a lot of work to unleash the bliss underneath the suffering.

The day came for the conference and I was excited to learn about new supernatural techniques. After experiencing such bliss and happiness with Arathi Ma, I assumed that more of the same would come from the weekend workshop.

The first day we learned the techniques of the Eight Brocade from a lady I will call Betty Lin. She was knowledgeable in the exercises and she was strict about how to perform them. In one instance she beckoned one middle-aged lady to the stage. The lady was in questionable shape and had struggled with the movements.

Betty Lin insisted that the exercises were simple and decided to prove that it was so by bringing a student up on stage with her. Betty Lin then asked the woman to stand with her back towards her. Betty Lin then started to lift the woman's arms slowly behind her back. This would stretch the front muscles of the shoulders, opening up the meridians therefore leading to greater health. I knew that what Betty said was true, but it was also clear that this "volunteer" was not ready for the degree of "Chi Gongness" imposed on her.

The arms lifted, the woman's face twisted, and not long after, a sound came from her that could only be described as a screech. Betty Lin insisted that all was fine, and let the "volunteer" retreat from the stage in pain. I was aware that there were many different types of gurus, and I was sure in those moments that Betty Lin was different from Arathi Ma. Betty Lin's teachings were useful to me; I felt great doing the exercises, and I was sure that even though Betty Lin's style of teaching appeared cruel, that some higher healing, whether it was emotional or physical, was taking place for the "volunteer" and everyone else involved.

Another such master that I will call Mr. Lee proposed that he could heal many elements using a combination of Chi Gong and acupuncture. I steadfastly agreed that this was possible, but was amazed to find how this man went about his practice. He would have as many as twenty to thirty people sit in a circle and he would move through them like a whirlwind, sticking them with acupuncture needles. The entire session would last an hour or more and I'm sure that many received results. By watching him, I realized that it was also apparent that he was an energetic master of a different sort than Arathi Ma. He wielded energy in order to create a specific result in the physical body; his highest agenda wasn't to free one from the suffering of the mind, but to free them from the suffering of the body. I also remembered Arathi Ma's words, "All arms of an octopus lead to the center." I fully believed that Mr. Lee had spiritual power, but it was clear that he wielded it in a different way.

The weekend Chi Gong intensive was also a successful experience for me. I learned that Chi Gong was a great spiritual practice with too many benefits to list and in some ways it was not so different than the path that I was already on. Chi Gong taught exercises to harness energy and energy is what we all were. There were many vibrations of energy and each vibration had different benefits and advantages. The weekend taught me to discard nothing and use all techniques towards finding happiness.

The day after the conference I called my girlfriend to share the excitement of my vacation with her. I had visited some of the relatives over the weekend and rediscovered more of my roots. She reaffirmed our differences by meeting my enthusiastic stories with a gentle, "Good for you" or "That's great." As was the case most of the time, the most exciting experiences of my life bored her to death. I can't say that I was over enthusiastic about the daily goings on in her world either. Although I still loved her, we were growing apart.

Rick's Healing

Days later after arriving back home to good old Maple Ridge, life returned to normal. Or at least, as normal as it could possibly be since Jamie had introduced me to Arathi Ma. If you don't believe me, then just ask any one of the other people he sent to see her.

One particular instance comes to mind. A year or so earlier, Jamie -- being as insistent as only he could be – suggested that a friend of ours named Rick go to see Arathi Ma. Rick was struggling with finding his life's purpose, as was the case with many of us in the western capitalistic world, and Jamie thought it would be good for Rick to seek Arathi Ma's guidance.

Rick was not one to see psychics or spiritual healers. He had little use for them. Many were frauds and charlatans and ones that weren't would only share what his destiny was and that was of no use to him – he didn't believe in fate and didn't want any part of it. On that premise, I agreed with him. Jamie then informed him that Arathi Ma was not a psychic or a doomsayer, but a healer that would connect him with his inner wisdom. If Rick got in touch with his inner wisdom then he would be better able to find his happiness.

Jamie, of course, had convinced another Rick of his stupidity, and off he went to Arathi Ma -- it seemed that Jamie had caught Rick and I in the same trap.

"Even the smartest of academics don't make judgments on something they have no experience in," Jamie would say. "Try (insert Jamie's solution for your failing life here) as an experiment for yourself."

Now, I don't know about you, but when something in your life isn't working, and someone approaches you with that argument, it's pretty much impossible to say "no" to trying whatever solution they have in store for you without looking like a close-minded jerk.

To make things worse, Jamie would then follow up the debate with doing something nice for you, like buying you lunch, giving you a book, or taking you to a movie. He was good at opening people up, although I doubt he ever realized it. I think it was because his convincing arguments didn't come from a place of selfishness; after all, he had nothing to gain from it. He convinced people to open up purely from a position of service to remove someone's ignorance and stubbornness from their lives. To confirm this further, Jamie was also a Naturopath known for referring his clients with regularity to other practitioners if there was the slightest doubt in his ability to heal them.

Rick returned from his session with Arathi Ma and sat down with Jamie to discuss it. Rick had learned something interesting, since having a seizure in the dentist chair as a child he had a healthy phobia of dentists. Well, not dentists in general, but in the needles they poked into his mouth. During the seizure, he had experienced a flashback of some sort. He had a vision of a car accident. In the vision he sat in the back seat of a car while a large truck smashed into it. His perspective then changed, and he gazed upon the accident from above to see the car in a crumpled mess.

Arathi Ma shared that his vision had been one of his past lives.

She also shared that his energetic system was running out of balance – all of the chakras were spinning backwards. This wasn't a surprise to him, as he had struggled with a variety of health problems, from kidney complications to allergic reactions to a variety of foods and airborne particles. She corrected his energetic system and informed him that he would experience some discomfort later that evening while his system balanced itself out.

It wasn't long into the discussion with Jamie when Rick expressed some of that discomfort. He complained of flu-like symptoms, and asked if he could continue the conversation later on.

Hours passed and Jamie decided to visit Rick to see how he was doing. Jamie's jaw dropped when Rick answered the door. Rick's eyes were nearly swollen shut, and his teeth chattered with the chills. He informed Jamie that he had taken a number of Tylenol Three's to no end, and that if things got any worse he'd check into the hospital for some tests.

Rick steadfastly agreed in that moment that there was something to this spiritual stuff, and his body's reaction was proof of it.

In an important note, the experience that was Rick's was known as spiritual cleansing. Trauma whether it was emotional or spiritual was carried in our bodies. Everyone knew that stress could cause a tension headache or a pain in the neck, so it only stood to reason that emotions could affect us on other levels as well. It was my theory that Rick had carried the trauma of his past life car accident, and when Arathi Ma helped him release it, he felt the energy of the trauma as it left him. That was the nature of spiritual cleansing. For example: if one wished to be free from depression, after performing spiritual disciplines to help the malady, the depression would often get worse before it got better. It was akin to spiritual vomiting. It was impossible to rid a substance from the body without feeling it first, whether it was from elimination of waste or a cough or a sneeze, and it was the same with energy. Emotions and traumas were another form of energy with an entirely new set of physical sensations and symptoms accompanying them.

I wasn't sure if Rick understood what had transpired, but I knew that his session with Arathi Ma had cleared a major blockage of suffering from his inner being. If it hadn't been cleared, I wasn't sure what would have happened to him, but I would bet my life on it that releasing the energetic trauma had averted a major health problem of some kind.

The Move

The time for my session came and Arathi Ma and I were reunited at last. She greeted me with a warm smile and a hug.

The satisfaction with myself showed in my smile. "I think I'm ready. I performed the exercises everyday since you taught them to me -- sometimes twice."

Arathi Ma's gaze grew distant as she scanned my aura. She then nodded. "You look clean enough. Are you sure you want this?"

I couldn't understand why I wouldn't want enlightenment sooner, so I nodded. "Of course, why wouldn't I want to speed things up?"

"After receiving the Shaktipat your life won't be the same. Lessons in life are learned at certain times. This will make that process happen faster. In other words, anything in your life that has to change for your spiritual wellbeing will change, whether you want it to or not."

I thought for a moment. I couldn't think of anything to worry about. My life was reasonably good. I performed my spiritual disciplines, ate healthy. I didn't drink, smoke, or do drugs. Everything was in alignment with my soul.

How little I knew.

"I'm ready," I said, the ignorance of a child in my words.

As a footnote, if you have plans in life and ask for a Shaktipat, throw the plans in the garbage. Come to think of it, don't just throw them in the garbage. Find a crate full of grenades, tie a string around all the pins, throw yourself and your plans in, and give the string a healthy pull. This might give you some idea of what happens after a Shaktipat. At least, that was my experience. In the end, of course, it was all for the better, I just didn't see it at the time.

I cannot describe the initiation that took place after due to its dangerous nature. I had Arathi Ma, a true guru, to guide me through the Shaktipat process. A person attempting the process without the guidance of a guru could cause a lot of damage to himself.

What I will share is that the initiation known as the Shaktipat involves the sacred process of raising the spiritual energy that sits at the base of the spine. When this process is started in a seeker, the energy continues upward until enlightenment is reached. This, of course, is true for all spiritual seekers, but think of this initiation as a turbo boost to the entire process.

I remember seeing small white clouds of energy flying in all directions from Arathi Ma. I saw this with my open eyes and it was as real to me as seeing a fly or a piece of dust. This energy was not either of these of course. The clouds were about an inch in diameter and when Arathi Ma spoke I had to laugh and apologize.

Arathi Ma tilted her head in a blend of curiosity and humor. "What is it?"

"I'm sorry. I see all this stuff flying off of you. It's very distracting. You speak and white puffs of energy are flying all over the place. It reminds me of someone speaking with their mouth full."

She laughed. "Sorry, it's what happens when I raise my Shakti."

I shook my head and smirked. "Every time I think I've seen everything, you do something new."

She grew a little more serious. "Isn't that great? The universe is never the same. Every moment is different. Never chase experiences because they will always be fresh and new. Just be. By the way, how are you feeling now?"

I had received my initiation only a few moments earlier, but I could not say that I felt anything abnormal. Nothing at all. Maybe a little boost in energy, more alert maybe, but that was about it.

"Good. Wasn't so bad," I said. I had expected something more powerful. Perhaps I was further along in my spiritual disciplines than I had thought.

Arathi Ma had told me that the initiation would change my life, but so far so good. No loud thunderclaps. No lightning bolts blasting through the ceiling of the office. No pavement rumbling, building-demolishing earthquakes. I decided all was good. Although I didn't have a blissful experience like I had during the Arut Perum Jothi initiation, I didn't have a bad experience either -- like insanity, which was known to happen in some people who had their Kundalini raised at a pace too fast for them to handle.

Yup, I was good. I bid Arathi Ma goodbye, and said that I would see her next week. Over the next few days, I went about my usual routine: training clients in the morning and two of my fulltime clients in the afternoon. At this point in my personal training business, my morning appointments had stalled to two a week and I was largely dependent upon my two full time clients that trained in the afternoon. They were the majority of my business.

One week after the initiation with Arathi Ma, I lost both of them. The two fulltime clients were brothers and worked in the same business. Their business had slowed and due to the nature of the increasing Canadian dollar, their American export business dwindled. They decided that it was best to cut their personal expenses at that point, and there I was suddenly without my fulltime income.

Coincidence? Perhaps, but I couldn't ignore the fact that this had happened when I was in the most vulnerable place. I usually had a few thousand dollars tucked away for emergencies such as these, but when I went on the trip with my father, I had missed work, and I was forced to use my meager savings for my car payment, phone, and insurance. There was less than a few hundred dollars in my account and next month's payments were coming quick. I was worried. What made it all worse was the fact that I could no longer afford to see Arathi Ma.

I admit to a little self-pity that day. It felt as I was being punished for going away with my father. Had I worked during that time, I would have had at least a few hundred more dollars to take me through the next month's bills.

The self-pity passed after a few hours at the gym. I continued my mantra practice, confident that Lakshmi would get me through my dilemma.

A week passed and no clients called and my financial dilemma continued. What made things worse, much worse, was the fact that my father was particularly irritated one day. I remember the conflict started when my father complained about coffee grounds in the sink – they hadn't been washed down properly. At the time I was in the midst of making the coffee, so it was understandable to me that there would be a mess until I was done. This was not in congruence with his point of view, so the conflict continued.

I snapped at my father, and after the words came from my mouth, I felt guilty about it. My father wasn't himself. Since leaving work he had experienced a number of emotional ups and downs that I could only describe as Post Traumatic Stress symptoms.

Of course, my mother came to my father's aid by throwing a few comments my way. I don't know whether it was my guilt about snapping at my father or if I was particularly irritated that day, but I exploded at my mother with a few expletives that I won't write here. I can only say that the words came out before I had a chance to censor them. The whole tirade unfolded before me and it was like I was watching the entire thing without any control over it. Something was up.

Well, hello there, Shaktipat. That's where you've been.

Another part of me knew that suppressing the outbursts would only make things worse, although logically I cannot say how that made sense.

It is said that that Kundalini energy sits at the base of the spine. It is known as a serpent or the divine mother. It is coiled three and half times and when it is activated, and the timing is right, it will uncoil like a spring and strike.

And strike it had.

More words were exchanged, tempers flared, and that day after returning from doing my spiritual disciplines in the park, I found all my stuff nicely tossed into three garbage bags and a suitcase – the same suitcase I had used for my trip to Newfoundland -- on the front porch. For some people, this would not be devastating. For me, it was like my life had ended. I distinctly remember a sensation akin to being thrown from a bridge. It felt like even though I was capable of walking, that the earth was no longer below me. It was not a metaphor. It really felt that way.

When life's struggles came up, for as long as I could remember I could depend on my family. It seemed, however, that was not the truth. At least not anymore.

My mother knew that money was short for me, especially after taking time off to travel with my ailing father. What made things worse was I had nowhere to go. At the time my brother, Jamie, lived in a one-bedroom apartment that he shared with his girlfriend. I knew Jamie would let me sleep on his couch, but I had no wish to add stress between him and his girlfriend. Besides, this was my problem. After all, I was in this predicament because I hadn't went to work and got a normal job like my father had asked me to do numerous times. I had also asked for the Shaktipat.

I couldn't live with my girlfriend either. She lived with her parents and her two brothers while she attended nursing school. There was no room for me there, nor was I eager to share my embarrassment with them. After all, I was in my early thirties. Wasn't that the age where little things like career and independence were figured out? My entire life I believed it was so and I had tortured myself continually for it. I had no wish to add fuel to the fire of my self-flagellation by disappointing my girlfriend's parents as well.

I also started to believe that this entire situation and how I was dealing with it was proof that my belief in happiness was flawed. And that there was a possibility that I had been misguided from a place of naïve stupidity. I was beginning to believe that making money should have been my highest priority after all.

Maybe my father's right, I thought.

An old conversation I had with my father rushed to the forefront of my mind. Dad was lecturing me about the "way the world was." I was off pursuing the sport of drug free bodybuilding. Five years later and a shelf full of trophies, I was still broke. I stuck to my principles however, and still searched for purpose and passion in my life.

"There's no such thing as purpose and happiness," Dad said.

"How can there be no such thing? There are people that love their work," I said. Hope was in my words, but I wasn't sure if I believed them anymore.

"They're lucky, but that isn't how life is. Life is suffering. You do what you have to do to live, and then take care of your family."

"What about happiness?" I said. "What about fun?"

"I don't know where you got this idea of fun and happiness from. I've never been happy my entire life."

This was a version of a conversation we had shared a number of times. My father sacrificed everything for those around him, but never thought of his own happiness.

My father had grown up in a poor home. A home where he shared a bed with five brothers. A home where one of his happiest moments was receiving a piece of fruit for Christmas. A home where he had to break the ice in the toilet before he used the washroom in the morning. Many days they went with nothing to eat. How could happiness be possible when starvation loamed?

Knowing this, my dad pursued what he knew as the opposite of starvation, which to him was security, and he pursued it almost to his death. Happiness had nothing to do with his view on life. Protecting his family and himself from starvation, the greatest pain he had ever felt, was his highest agenda.

I wondered if in the coming months I was about to experience what it felt like to not have enough to eat. I drove around Maple Ridge, wondering where I was going to sleep. I worried about everything, my father's viewpoints on life swirling in my mind. On some level, he was right, and I admit to trying to buy into his way of life, but in the end I couldn't bring myself to pursue security instead of passion.

I just couldn't wrap my mind around his way of thinking, although it made perfect sense in my present situation. After all, he was right on one level. Stability could definitely serve as a support for happiness to flourish. If I had a stable job, then changing my place of residence would not have been so stressful. The only problem was that every time I chose to pursue stability over happiness in my life, it hadn't worked out anyway. So at some point I said, "Screw it." I figured that if I did something I liked and didn't make any money, at least I had fun doing it. If I pursued stability, I might actually achieve it, but for what? Most often the energy spent in that direction created so much stress and unhappiness that life became the pure shit that my dad made it out to be. I was sure that there was a middle ground in there somewhere, but I also firmly believed that it was up to me to find my own balance in it.

I decided to push away the conditioning of society and my upbringing. If life was nothing but survival, then what was the point? I couldn't bear to live that way. I parked the car and felt sorry for myself. I hadn't been able to find my balance so far. Would I ever?

Perhaps, I was a man that wasn't meant for the world after all. I had failed my parents by not finding my financial success. Failed Arathi Ma by not holding my place of bliss and happiness amidst the drama of my life.

I spent a good amount of time at my pity party before a thought occurred to me. No matter what happened, no matter where I slept or what I did in the next few days, even if I starved to death, nothing could take away the experiences that Arathi Ma had given to me. She had given me proof that happiness existed regardless of the ups and downs of life. She gave me proof that it could endure through all of it. The peace and bliss inside us could transcend anything and it wasn't dependent on anything. I only had to rediscover it.

Thoughts of Arathi Ma meandered through my mind for only a few moments before a smile returned to my face. I decided to call her and inform her of the interesting turn of events in my life. After all, she had warned me that something in my life would shift. I was sure that she would be interested in finding out exactly what *had* shifted.

When she answered my call I told her of what had transpired. She was surprised at first and apologized for how things had unfolded. "There's no way to tell how the Divine Mother will reset the course of your life," she said.

"I know. I must have been really messed up because it feels like my life is falling apart. I don't know what I'm going to do. How I'm going to eat? Where am I going to live?"

Arathi Ma's voice was like medicine to my pain. "I know. It's hard. I've been through similar times on my journey. Just know that God will take care of you. There is a plan at work and it's impossible for you to see it right now."

"I know and thank you," I said, tears welling in the corners of my eyes; the fear and isolation was too much for me to bear.

She hesitated. "I know it's quite a commute to Vancouver, but if you need something to eat, there's always food in my fridge."

Gratitude overwhelmed me. I broke down a little in that moment, but I think I hid it well. I had no intention of imposing on Arathi Ma and taking her food, but knowing that she cared was more than enough to give me courage to go on. Arathi Ma, the person that had done so much for me, given me reasons to live when I had none at all, was now helping me piece together the crumbling pieces of my failure of a life. My life's failures were all my fault, my doing, for not being what I had been raised to be – a responsible, money-making adult – and yet there she was forgiving me for me my failures, accepting me for who I was. It was too much for my heart to take. I thanked her, and reasserted my will to live, to go on.

Arathi Ma was the wisest most magical person I had ever met, and if she said that I was okay just the way I was, then I was damn well okay. Everyone else could kiss my ass.

With my new conviction on life, I decided to phone some of my friends to see if anyone needed a roommate. My phone calls revealed that a fellow bodybuilding acquaintance from the gym was indeed in need of one. I could move in right away, and he was okay if I was a little late on the rent. His name was Mike. He was a serious amateur bodybuilding competitor and his life rotated strongly around training and running his bodybuilding supplement store. The store sold protein powders and vitamins to most of the sports minded people in town. He was, in fact, in the midst of expanding his business to a neighboring community.

I wish to express gratitude for his help. If it weren't for him, I'm not sure where I would have slept.

That night, I have to admit that "moving in" was a little humiliating. While most people moved into their new residence with furniture, clothing, and kitchen appliances, I had three black garbage bags and a suitcase filled with an assortment of clothes, books, and bathroom items. Mike's eyes widened when I dumped my belongings onto the bedroom floor. It was clear that everything had been packed in a most violent manner.

"Rough day," Mike said, with the slightest hint of a smirk.

I ignored the comment and scanned the room. It was small, but it had a big window decorated with a set of horizontal blinds. I was thankful to see that the room also had a bed.

Mike followed my gaze to the small bed. "Don't worry. We can move it out when you bring your furniture in." He had clearly misread my thoughts.

"No. I'll use it if that's alright with you." I couldn't imagine going back to my parent's house to get my furniture. Actually, at that point I couldn't imagine ever seeing them again.

Mike scanned my belongings strewn about the floor. "Hasty move, huh?" Mike said, smirking again.

"You could say that," I said, my face reddening under his gaze.

He was taking a little too much pleasure in my pain, but I decided it wasn't the right time to punch him in the mouth. I had had enough drama for one day. I was sure however, that it wouldn't be long before everyone at the gym knew how I had showed up on his doorstep. Mike was a guy that couldn't resist the temptation of a good gossip-fest, and I was sure that my situation would make the upcoming week's headlines.

Mike then showed me my bathroom, the shared kitchen, the living room, the entertainment room, and the sun deck. He informed me which cupboards in the kitchen were mine and oriented me with the locations of dishes, cups, and utensils.

Some of my panic started to fade. The house seemed like a nice place to live. In all, it was over three thousand square feet in size and the sundeck had a beautiful view of the mountains. In some ways it was a noticeable step up from my former lifestyle for the same amount of rent. What made things even better was that it was very likely that I'd have the place to myself, seeing as Mike was most often at work, and the roommate that rented the downstairs was rarely home.

Perhaps I would be okay after all. How many people could rent a room in a beautiful house without a damage deposit, or any money at all for that matter? God was indeed helping me through the charity of others.

I went to visit my girlfriend that night and although I hadn't shared my situation with her parents their expressions showed that she had. My girlfriend's mother, Susan, gave me the most pitiful look. I imagined that puppies about to be euthanized also received that same look before meeting their end.

Susan tilted her head and gave me the warmest smile, sharing her spiritual warmth with me. "Is there anything you need, dear?"

I shook my head. I was lying of course. I didn't have anything.

She saw right through it and proceeded with a line of questioning that prevented further lies. "Do you have a pillow? Towels? Blankets?"

I tried to lie and hesitated too long. I was a horrible liar.

Susan was off to gather the items. She handed them to my girlfriend and then gave me the most serious gaze. "If you need anything, you let us know."

I almost broke down again. I have heard many horror stories involving mother-in-laws, but Susan was nothing like any of those other mothers I had heard about. Any man lucky enough to call her his mother-in-law was indeed blessed. Susan was a most caring person, and even though I had definitely *not* been successful in bringing happiness and stability to her daughter, she still showed me the warmest of feelings and compassion. My girlfriend's father was much the same. They were not rich or well off, but they fed me more times than I can count without a thought of it. Most often I couldn't even leave the house without Susan following me with a dish full of leftovers to take with me.

Again, God took care of me through these beautiful people. Susan and Robert will always be in my prayers for the kindness they showed me despite my struggle to find myself.

I bid my girlfriend and Susan goodnight. I was humbled by their kindness: I know that I did not deserve it. My girlfriend and I had grown apart very much in the last few years, and I sensed a change was coming.

I spent that night, in my new home, gazing at the moon. A mixed bundle of emotions moved through me. Gratitude for the kindness I had received. Guilt for not deserving it. And fear for what was to come. In those moments, I had the sense that I didn't know anything. I didn't know what to do. I only knew that I felt alone in doing it.

Separate Ways

Through a stroke of luck (or Lakshmi's support) Mike informed me that his new store could use a little help. I met with his partner, who was also a friend of mine from years back, and pitched an idea to him. The agreement was that I would workout with him at the local gym, while handing out coupons for his struggling vitamin store. For the service of promoting his business three days a week, he would pay me five hundred dollars a month. It was enough for me to pay my rent and have a hundred dollars left over for gas for the commute.

For almost a year, I had chanted mantras for attracting abundance, and although I attracted many things, money wasn't one of them. So far I had been kicked out of my place of residence, lost most of my personal training clients, and had little hope of any abundance coming my way anytime soon. It seemed that Lakshmi had other work for me to do first.

It turned out that Steve (the friend that owned the newly opened vitamin store) had a number of concerns in his life that he wanted to work out. Through a series of conversations, I convinced him to see Arathi Ma.

As I continued my work with Steve, he shared some of his experiences and I can say that they were amazing. In one such story he told me that he had asked Arathi Ma to help him with his busy mind. The busy mind would lead to bouts of anxiety. The anxiety would dominate his life and then his digestion would be affected in quite an extreme way. Many days he complained of acid reflux and heartburn. The doctors couldn't figure out what was wrong with him.

Steve said that Arathi Ma asked him to lie on the table while she placed her hands on both sides of his head. His mind started to "get really busy" and he experienced an electrical shock. Steve jolted from his relaxation to a state of wide-eyed sobriety. "What the hell was that?" he had said. He told me that it was like a lightning bolt had suddenly passed through his brain. "A lot of my anxiety left after that," he said.

Steve had many other sessions with Arathi Ma and I was sure the divine guided his path as closely as it guided mine. After all, my misfortune – or fortune depending on how one looked at it -- forced our paths together. I had connected him to Arathi Ma and he had helped me continue my personal journey by helping me with a job.

I continued working with Steve and personal training my dwindling client list. I was broke, but I managed to scrape by through the charity of others. Jamie's girlfriend, Tara, fed me many times and was all too happy to give me Tupperware containers filled with her good cooking. I want to be clear. I didn't get by on my own. Many people helped me in their own large and small ways.

My father and mother had tried calling me several times, but I wasn't ready to speak to them yet. Although the episode that had happened between us was clearly my fault, they left their apologies for how things had transpired on my voice mail.

One day my father called and I picked up. He said that all was fine and that everything had gotten all blown out of proportion. "You should come back now," he said.

I thanked him, but refused. Everything needed to happen the way it had. It was time I tested my faith in life. Besides, lessons started to reveal themselves to me. For instance, I had been out of the house for two weeks and it had not been that bad. Actually, I felt kind of free. No one could tell me what the right or wrong decision was, and all my explorations of life were mine to discover. And seeing as my roommates were most often out of the house, I was free to practice my spiritual exercises without anyone telling me that I was "Om-ing too loud."

I organized a time that I could pick up the rest of my stuff, and couldn't leave the house without my father firmly pressing two hundred dollars into my hand. I tried to give it back, but it seemed that he wouldn't sleep that night if I didn't take it. Like I said, my Lakshmi mantras had produced abundance, but not in the million dollar way I would have liked. Instead, Lakshmi's energy had manifested itself as love and help from others – even the very people that I accidentally mistreated. It seemed that if I failed, people were there to offer their forgiveness for my shortcomings and help me in spite of them. Only now, I also had freedom and fewer conditions attached to such aid.

Soon a month passed, and another truth revealed itself to me. In one of my daily visits to my girlfriend's house, the differences of our paths became too obvious to me. Our conversations had dwindled to a few words, although genial, and I could feel her boredom as well as my own. She had even turned to me several times in the last few weeks and asked, "I think we should be friends, don't you?"

I ignored the question because I had chalked up my dissatisfaction with the relationship as my own personal flaws. I figured that with enough spiritual work and personal reflection that I would somehow fix myself. The more spiritual work I performed, the more the fixing became elusive. It all came to an end one night when we were watching television together. She had done nothing wrong. We weren't fighting or annoying each other in any way, but a terrible uncomfortable feeling manifested in my sternum. No matter which way I moved or adjusted my position, the feeling didn't go away. It was a feeling of urgency. I had to go. I told my girlfriend that and I left.

The next day we had a discussion on the phone and it ended in us parting ways. Sadness played a large part of the discussion. We had been together for eight years and trusted each other implicitly. She was a good friend and good person. I did not want to waste any more of her time and the feeling was mutual on her part.

So it seemed that my transition, or the destruction of my life, was complete. Now I was truly by myself to make my own decisions. I didn't have to worry about marriage, buying a house, or even having a career. I could live in a cardboard box if I had to. After all, the trappings of responsibility were the things that came as a package deal with having a girlfriend. The inevitable questions would come up: How are you going to support a family? When are you going to have kids? Oh yeah, and don't forget to prepare for retirement. I had heard all of these questions from everyone around me a million times, but the worst part was that the questions never left my head either. Part of me must have still bought into the importance of them even though they caused me unhappiness. I decided that the only way I'd be able to let the thoughts go was if I was by myself with no one around me to reinforce them.

I was in a new chapter in my life. I was no longer distracted by the needs and beliefs of everyone else. I could finally start to find out who I was and what I wanted, and I knew that if I stuck with my spiritual disciplines, the truth would come to me.

Love

I couldn't afford to book any healing sessions with Arathi Ma in the first month in my new home. I did, however, stay in touch with her through email and the odd phone call from time to time. I also attended Satsang with her on Friday evenings. Satsang was a guided meditation in search of truth. Arathi Ma would discuss various topics on finding one's true self and then guide us through a meditation. Her meditations were challenging at times and I sometimes felt like I was the balloon being held out the window of a speeding car. It was common for people to drop off into sleep half way through the meditation and I admit to a few nods of my own.

Arathi Ma explained that one of the goals of meditation was to bring our unconsciousness conscious. "We are all enlightened in our sleep," she said. "In our deepest sleeps – the sleeping beyond dream state

-- we are unaware of our egos and our conditioning. That is when we are ourselves – pure consciousness."

When Arathi Ma dragged the unconscious parts of us to a conscious state many of us fell asleep because we could not hold the state while awake. Of course, staying awake was the goal. Another way she referred to it was being in a state of presence. We were conscious and engaging in the world with no thought, unless we so chose to have a thought. "Many of us don't realize it," she said, "but we are controlled by thoughts that are not even our own; they are only patterns floating around inside us dominating our every action and emotion without our knowledge of it."

Every Friday was Satsang day and it started at 6:00 pm. I wished that I could have afforded a session with Arathi Ma too, but my money situation still floundered. Of course, that was when Lakshmi came to the rescue. She must have known that I missed Arathi Ma in the largest way and it seemed that Joselyn, the lady who owned the house where Arathi Ma worked, saw it too.

One Friday, Joselyn called me and asked if I wanted an appointment with Arathi Ma. I told her that I couldn't afford it, but would see her at the mediation. Joselyn then informed me what was on the menu for lunch that day, and then extended me an invitation.

The invitation was too great to ignore. I wasn't one to pass up a free lunch, and I said as much to Joselyn, but the real reason for accepting invitation was obvious to everyone except for me. Joselyn saw it in the way I looked at Arathi Ma, the way I clung to every word she said, the way I smiled every time Arathi Ma laughed.

I had read that gurus had a special energy around them that made them attractive to the true seeker of God. I had chalked my intense attraction to her as just that. I knew that I loved her, but my love for her was totally pure. This was not the love I had experienced in the relationships of my past. I had no urge for sexual union or anything like that. I just loved Arathi Ma intensely for who she was. It was the most unconditional love I had ever felt for anyone.

That's why it hit me like a ton of bricks when I realized that my love for her had evolved into something more complete.

I remember a conversation I had with Joselyn. I felt guilty and shameful. What kind of asshole fell in love with his spiritual guru?

"I can't believe it. I feel so guilty. I'm not supposed to like her this way. I must be going through some type of spiritual shift or something."

Joselyn chuckled. "No, I don't think so. You love her. What's wrong with that?"

I was confused. "I feel like such an idiot. How long has this been going on? Why didn't you tell me?"

I thought of my ex girlfriend. Had my emotions somehow betrayed her as well? Had I started to love Arathi Ma a long time ago? I decided that if I had, I didn't know it at the time.

"You should talk to Arathi Ma about it. Maybe she can tell you what's going on," Joselyn said. I could almost hear the deviousness in her words.

Talk to Arathi Ma about it.

That's what I'll do, I thought in the most sarcastic way. *Right. That'll solve everything.*

It seemed like the shifting of my life was not yet finished.

The Final Healing

I decided to scientifically approach the irrationality of my emotions. Loving my guru was some sort of phase. A shift. I would pass through it like all other things, I only had to apply the techniques to allow it to happen.

Simple really.

The time came when I scraped enough money together to see Arathi Ma for another healing session. I called her on the phone and gave her a lowdown on what was going on.

"I'm feeling irrational stuff," I said.

The concern in her voice apparent as always. "What kind of stuff."

"Love."

She laughed. "What's wrong with that?"

"For my guru. That's what's wrong with it. Must be a Kundalini thing or an energetic shift." I rambled on a whack load of justifications that all sounded equally justified.

"Oh." Arathi Ma hesitated. "That happens sometimes. A seeker sees God in the guru and then falls in love with the energy. All perfectly normal. Just enjoy it because it is only a manifestation of your urge to unite with the Divine."

Relief swept through me. I wasn't a jerk after all. It was a perfectly normal phenomenon associated with the dramatic shifts in awareness I had experienced and the euphoria that went with it. I must have been mixing up the euphoria with the feeling of love.

Either way, no matter what it was, there was nothing to worry about.

Arathi Ma wasn't worried, so I didn't worry either.

I booked my session, eager to move the next step of my transformation. So far, most of my life had disintegrated, and although my meditations and spiritual experiences had increased, my life was a living car wreck from an egotistical point of view. I mean, scraping a hundred dollars together was a challenge, and I had little idea how I was going to use this new freedom I had found to become whoever it was I was supposed to be in this world. I knew that the struggle to find myself was a sign of my conditioning, but I just didn't know how to get rid of it.

Either way, I figured that things in my daily life had to look up soon. If this spiritual stuff was supposed to help someone in all areas of their life, then it only made logical sense that something positive would come my way soon, didn't it?

The next week I traveled to Arathi Ma's office for my appointment. We continued the appointment as usual by starting with, "Let's see how your chakras are doing today."

I lay on the table and she ran energy into my body, filling up my system where it was needed. I think it was about the time when we were halfway done the session when I felt my arms start to burn. It wasn't the normal type of subtle heat that one experienced, but more like a burning tingle that danced up and down my arms. It started to run through my entire body, as if I had twenty cups of coffee intravenously run into my veins. The only difference was that I didn't feel jittery or shaky.

At the end of the session, I got off the table.

"How do you feel?" Arathi Ma said.

"Great. Energetic I guess."

Arathi Ma smiled, nodded, and gave a nonchalant, "Good."

I was on my way home, thinking that everything was okay. I had fixed my "problem" with the love nuisance and I felt great. When I arrived into Maple Ridge I went to the gym. That was when I started to feel that something was off.

I grabbed the weights off the wrack to warm up with some bench presses. Everything felt light to me. I grabbed heavier weights, and was surprised to hear myself grunt like an enraged beast. The thrill of victory flowed through my veins and if someone asked me to fight a grizzly bear with my naked hands, I'm not sure that I would have refused. Better yet, not only would I have accepted the challenge, but I was sure that after I was finished with the bear, I'd be picking my teeth with its discarded bones.

Yes, something strange was going on.

My friend, David, who was familiar with Arathi Ma's work, ran into me during my workout. I explained to him that I had just come from one of her healing sessions.

"I feel great. Like I could run through a wall," I said and I'm sure that the expression I wore matched that of a Wildman. "How do you feel, Dave? Looking good – this spiritual stuff is quite a rush – don't you think? Yup, I feel great."

David nodded and took a step backwards. His retreat was filled with trepidation, almost as if he was afraid that if he withdrew too fast that he'd encourage a wild beast to chase him. David's eyes were wide with fear when he spoke.

"You're freaking me out," he said. I guessed then that he then decided a quick retreat was best. He made a brisk about-turn and walked away as fast as his little yoga legs could take him.

I turned back to my war against the weights, every clank of the dumbbells filling me with exhilaration.

That night, I returned home from the gym, ate some chicken and rice for dinner, and then went outside on the sundeck to enjoy a cup of tea in the company of the setting sun. Arathi Ma was in the forefront of my mind. I could not get her out of my head. It was as if she spoke to me in my thoughts and her smiling image was ever-present in my mind. This sort of thing had been common for quite a while at this point, so I was used to it, but for some reason, this night it was even stronger than usual. I had been willing to ignore it before, but I couldn't ignore it any longer. I loved Arathi Ma. And it didn't look like it was going away anytime soon.

The feeling of exhilaration from my session with Arathi Ma continued to flow through my veins. It powered through my inhibitions and I no longer cared whether it was right or wrong to love Arathi Ma. I just did. And it was intense. The most deeply intense feeling of love that I had ever experienced. Love had hit me a few times in my life, and each time it was wonderful. The love for Arathi Ma was a whole other concept altogether. Love as I had experienced it, would feel warm and fuzzy, almost ticklish in the heart. Love for Arathi Ma was of another nature. Although the warm fuzzy feelings were also present, there was an intensity to it much deeper in my heart, in the very fiber of my being, that I never knew existed. I had to have her. I had to be around her. I could no longer accept the fact that I wasn't with her.

Every mantra I said, every meditation I performed, was filled with thoughts of her. I used every amount of my spiritual power, every amount of my love to pull her towards me.

And soon enough, it worked.

"I felt your soul wooing me," she said.

We spent our first date at the beach, gazing up at a cloud formation that reminded me closely of the deity, Ganapathi.

I pointed it out to Arathi Ma, and she smiled. "I think he had something to do with this."

Isolation

People always say, "Follow your heart." I listened to them. The few times in my life that my heart told me something, I followed it with a vengeance. The only problem was that my heart opened with the same rarity as a visitation from Haley's Comet. Well, because of this rarity, it was remarkably easy for me to see that my heart was demanding me to follow it now. And so I did.

The explosions came after.

I won't go into all the details because there are those that deserve their privacy, but let's just say that whole "follow your heart thing" has some fine print that I forgot to read. For one thing, following your heart does not mean that the journey afterward will be easy.

I thought that bringing a magical being like Arathi Ma into my family circle would be the happiest day of all of our lives. After all, in India when a guru entered the family circle it was celebrated.

It became very apparent that I did not live in India.

Arathi Ma ran a workshop shortly after we got together. Jamie and his girlfriend were in attendance and Arathi Ma decided that it would be a good time to tell them the good news.

Jamie went into shock and left. I received text messages from him telling me what kind of jerk I was and in one text message he said not to talk to him anymore. I had taken his guru away, changed his spiritual path forever. He would never forgive me.

I felt horrible, but there was nothing I could do to change what had happened. I couldn't understand where he was coming from. Honestly. I thought that there would be nothing better than have Arathi Ma at family dinners, telling us about the magical nature of the universe, performing miracles on a daily basis. I couldn't see what was so bad about that? I guess you could say that if "love was blind" then I was a bat.

It seemed that Arathi Ma had done her job. In India, it was common for gurus to cause mayhem and drama in every situation they entered all in the attempt to connect those involved to their true selves. My brother and I had shared an intense bond our entire lives as I'm sure most twin siblings do, and for us to go further in the discovery of ourselves, perhaps we needed time apart so that we didn't interfere in each other's process. Perhaps this was Arathi Ma's guru strategy although she'd never admit to any of it.

Either way, life was difficult. My tenuous ties to the family were sliced in half again. If I showed up to a family gathering, it ended up in an intense debate between my brother and I. My parents didn't want to take sides, but because of my brother's greater success and strong ability to argue his point to death, ultimately I'd get the "What were you thinking?" glare.

My answer to their question was: I didn't think at all. I only loved.

I commuted to Vancouver everyday to stay with Arathi Ma. It was a way to get away from the conflict and find myself again. In my entire adult life, I thought that if there was anyone I could depend on, it was my twin brother. Perhaps that was my mistake. Yoga taught me that there was no other, only the self. Jamie's actions only mirrored some part inside of me. I only didn't know what that part was.

The universe was teaching me something. I only didn't know what it was, and couldn't understand why learning it had to hurt so much.

I remembered the night Arathi Ma and I had decided to be a couple. I leaned over the balcony of her townhouse to gaze at the neighboring church. I should have known that trouble was brewing. A lightning storm tore across a pink and purple sky and thunder roared for three hours without a drop of rain. What made it even stranger was the fact that I saw movement in the sky above the golden dome of the church. I could only describe it as shadows streaking through the air. I asked Arathi Ma what the streaks were and she told me that they were souls attracted to the place of worship.

Although I didn't understand the meaning of the lightning bolts the night that I had seen them, I understood them then as I listened to the bustle of Vancouver traffic and the calls of seagulls. Our union had caused quite a commotion between my brother and I.

I hoped that everything would be okay.

Another one of my visions came that night. I woke up to see my brother hovering at the foot of my bed. His face changed into an East Indian man, then into himself again. He smiled at me. A smile so enthusiastic that his face scrunched up until it utterly changed into the face of a smiling Buddha.

I knew then that all was good. After all, the vision told me that my brother was a great spiritual master of some sort. All of this drama must have happened for some greater reason.

I admit that it was hard for me to understand how life with my family had become such a mess, but as history had taught me, from destruction came the birth of something new. I was sure that the appearance of my brother was a sign that all would be okay.

The first month of staying with Arathi Ma was a new and exciting experience. Many of those summer nights I spent upstairs, listening to the bustle of the city while the plum tree scented air wafted into the room.

Arathi Ma would go to bed early and I would stay up to watch television and then meditate. On the third night of staying in the townhouse I noticed that there was something else going on in Arathi Ma's residence. Now, I've had my experiences with seeing energy or spiritual fog, but this was even more pronounced than I was accustomed to. I would sit in the dim light of the setting sun and gaze around the room. Mist would move in organized patterns, or small pieces of white fluffy energy would dart horizontally through the air before my eyes. Let's just say that it didn't look like the workings of any wind or air phenomenon.

I decided that this Arathi Ma creature was magical indeed.

I wondered what it would be like to watch her sleep. Up until that point, because of her early bedtime, we had decided that I would sleep in another room to keep from waking her. My curiosity got the better of me one night and I snuck into her room. What I saw confused me, and put me in a state of awe at the same time.

She lay flat on her stomach, reminding me of the sleeping position of the average three-year-old. A cloud of milky energy surrounded her body. It was subtle, but it shimmered almost as if it was a mirage of some sort. It was as if she was bathed in mist. Little sparks darted in and out of it like tiny fireflies.

Up until that point, I had experienced the odd vision in meditation and seen some subtle energetic stuff with my physical eyes, but I couldn't say that I was gifted with spiritual sight. But yet, there I was, seeing the energy around her. Arathi Ma's right leg kicked and twitched, and I thought it best to leave so that I didn't wake her up.

The next morning I mentioned that I had snuck into her room to watch her sleep. I mentioned the fog and she just gave a nonchalant shrug. "Just energy stuff. Other balls of light flying around are the souls of my students trying to connect with me. I work on them at night to make sure their okay."

Now I don't know about you, but when you see something that isn't supposed to exist and you think it's the biggest discovery since fire and you express it to someone and they merely shrug it off, you feel like an idiot. Why didn't I know about this stuff before? Where the hell had I been for the last thirty years? Was I blind before or something?

"Oh," I said, dumbfounded with the casualness of her answer. "You sure kick a lot in your sleep." I smiled.

She sighed. "Yeah, it's the Kundalini energy. When it activates strongly it gets stuck where there are blockages. Lately, my right calf has been blocked up a bit."

Another night, after Arathi Ma went to bed, I performed some pranayama and then went into meditation. The particular type of pranayama that I performed that night was something called the Clearing Out Technique. It was a technique advocated by the guru, Namadeva, and it worked great for taking me into deep meditation.

I finished the breathing exercise and then sank deeper and deeper into a place of no-thought. Relaxation swept through me, and then an image so clear and beautiful appeared. A dark-haired woman with a smile as warm and loving as Arathi Ma's stood before me. She wore a dark green satin dress in East Indian fashion.

Lakshmi, I thought. I was sure of it. Only Lakshmi could have such warmth and love in her smile.

The vision disappeared and I somehow knew that she was telling me that my Lakshmi mantras had taken me to this new place in my life. It was only a little over a year ago that depression had dominated me, and it was then that I had prayed for magical experiences, for a solution to my unhappiness.

And there I was, on the top floor of the townhouse, experiencing and living what I had prayed for.

Another day, Arathi Ma and I returned from grocery shopping. We put the groceries away and I moved to the living room to slump into a chair for a rest, as was the custom after walking several blocks with our groceries. It was a tough day, my brother and I still weren't getting along, and news of my relationship with Arathi Ma circulated through her students and although some of them were happy for us, others were not at all.

I wiped my hand down my face and when I opened my eyes I noticed something near the couch. No. It was on the couch, a shimmering, mirage-like energy hovering above the cushions.

I pointed it out to Arathi Ma. I did this often. I was like a child pointing out every spiritual phenomenon that I noticed. I had to know if I was really seeing something or if my eyes were tricking me. It must have seemed incredibly juvenile to Arathi Ma, whose entire life was a spiritual experience, but she weathered my questions with good nature.

Arathi Ma closed her eyes and said, "Oh, it's one of my clients coming back to see me."

"Can't they just book a session?" I complained. This energetic visitation stuff was intruding on our personal life, and it was nice to have a conversation once in a while without Arathi Ma suddenly having to halt in mid-sentence and say, "So and so is trying to connect with me right now."

Arathi Ma shook her head. "No, he can't book a session because he's no longer with us. He passed away several years ago."

I slumped a little with guilt. "Oh." I turned to the mirage on the couch and talked to the image much like someone talked to an answering machine. "Hi, nice to meet you."

Arathi Ma grinned. "His energy is very powerful. He's giving our relationship his blessing."

I turned to the mirage. "Thank you."

There was no mistaking that something was in the room with us. I was humbled by his visitation and his message. It had come at a time when I very much needed it.

The mirage stayed for a moment longer and then faded.

"He's gone now." She turned to me and I thought she'd say something else about the amazing experience we had just had, but she only asked, "What're we having for dinner?"

Blessings

Soon Arathi Ma and I decided that it would be best to get an apartment. The rent in the townhouse was expensive and she wanted to be closer to her office. She soon found a place within walking distance of it. At the time I also decided to make a life for myself in Vancouver. After all, it didn't make much sense for me to commute to Maple Ridge for my dwindling client list.

I didn't have much to contribute to our situation so we ended up getting an apartment much smaller than I was used to. Moving from a three thousand square foot home to a small one-bedroom apartment was a shock to me.

In India, great spiritual masters migrated to the caves of the Himalayan Mountains. I, on the other hand, had migrated to a small one-bedroom apartment where I was forced to keep all of my belongings in a linen closet. I can't tell you how many mornings I struggled to find a pair of socks in that dark closet while towels and other linens attacked me from above. I could almost hear them yelling, "Geronimo!"

If I had any ideas of luxury, they were surrendered when I moved into my new home. Don't get me wrong; it was nice, but really small, too small for two people. Arathi Ma was also a light sleeper, so I decided to sleep on a mattress in the living room, so that I didn't disturb her.

I called my mattress the Dog Mat.

The Dog Mat was placed beside a single chair that faced my big screen television – the only possession that I had taken with me in my great spiritual pilgrimage to Vancouver. The table where we ate was also placed beside the chair; so basically I ate, slept, meditated, and watched television in an area of one square meter.

I was thankful, at least, for the adjoining balcony. Everyday I went outside and enjoyed the company of the trees that grew beside the apartment building. Their rustling leaves were music to me, and more than once I meditated upon them.

I learned to tolerate my surroundings, but I admit that I was an outdoor dog. And like any outdoor dog, I needed a yard to roam. I knew that this was something I had to deal with inside, rather than out, but still the boredom loomed.

I don't know how long it was before I realized that my excitement for life began to fade. Depression returned into my life, but what was even more confusing was that my mood would not stay in one state; some days it would shift into happiness or extreme love. In my past, I had experienced depression without any respite from it so at least, I thought, this was an improvement.

This shifting of moods continued back and forth with depression coming in even more powerful waves. It wasn't long before the gloominess lasted several days at a time before I was given a break from it.

I don't know how long this went on before I realized what was happening. I knew of the phenomenon of spiritual cleansing or of clearing out mental patterns. I had experienced it when I had first started my mantra disciplines. And I also knew that it was common knowledge in spiritual circles that when one practiced spiritual work, the issues that one sought to resolve got worse before getting better.

What I hadn't thought about was that when one was in the company of a guru for extended periods of time, the spiritual cleansing phenomenon happened at an exponential rate. That was why it was common for thousands of followers to sit at a guru's feet to receive his Darshan. I had disregarded the possibility of Arathi Ma's energy affecting me so strongly because I had been okay around her for several months. I thought I was immune to it, but I had made one critical mistake. I hadn't factored in the variable of *duration of time* in her energetic field.

So that was why my depression was getting worse. I was cleansing it out of my system along with boredom, anxiety, and a shopping list of other patterns I had.

It was difficult.

Many things passed through my mind during this time. Had I made a mistake? How could I feel this badly if all this spiritual stuff worked? Had I made a mistake with Arathi Ma?

Memory after memory flashed through my mind. Miracles had happened to me because of her. Love beyond anything I ever imagined had come to me because of her. It was the truth. It was uncontestable. I decided that anything that happened to me from that point on had to be merely a spiritual cleanse, an illusion. And no matter how bad the depression got, I had to charge my way through it. So far, Arathi Ma had steered me in the right direction. I couldn't lose faith in her now; even when my mind wanted to come in and destroy everything I had worked toward.

Arathi Ma helped this process every step of the way, of course. And even though the depression was always with me, she still had the most magical way of giving me reprieve from its grip. As was the custom,

I'd perform my mantras in my chair as I watched television, waves of gray emotions moving through me as I chanted. In that moment, I'd decide that nothing could take me out of the grayness, and that was when Arathi Ma would come into the room and kneel before me. She'd slump onto my lap, smile, and stare into my eyes. The innocence and affection in her expression would be too powerful to ignore, and I could not resist giving her a hug. And every time I did, warmth spread through me, easing my emotional burden.

She continued to guide me using a series of techniques, but most importantly, we talked and connected. Everyday we spoke of various spiritual practices, how they were applied, and why. At the time, mind yogic techniques only frustrated me, and she knew it, so she conquered me by helping me learn to use my heart. Many nights, we just held each other without speaking, without saying anything or having to do anything. She taught me awareness of my chakras and how to connect them to hers.

And in between the aggressive cleanses, the spiritual experiences continued.

One day, my brother and I formed a tentative truce. We agreed to disagree on a number of things and he came downtown for a visit. I think he was more disappointed than I was with my living conditions as his gaze took in the miniscule apartment. We sat around -- I on the Dog Mat,

Jamie and Arathi on the only available chairs – discussing mantras and healing techniques. I performed my mantras silently in my head as the conversation continued and only a few minutes into the discussion a high-pitched sound reverberated in my ears.

I stuck my finger in my ear and wiggled it around, wondering what the heck was going on, but the ringing didn't go away. I interrupted the conversation and asked Arathi Ma what I was experiencing.

She closed her eyes, and then said, "Tara has come to visit."

"Jamie's girlfriend?"

"No." She shook her head. "Tara, the deity known in Buddhism. It is because of the Om Mani Padme Hum mantra you've been practicing. You must have reached some sort of proficiency with it."

The ringing transformed into a light relaxation that swept through my body, and I couldn't help but scan the air around the apartment. I couldn't see anything out of the ordinary, but I felt great. I gave my thanks and hoped that Tara would visit me again.

The blessings continued to come. Most often they manifested as overwhelming feelings of relaxation or comfort in different parts of my body. I cannot say where they came from or from whom they came, but I sure as heck didn't want them to go away. Most often they came when I sat in my chair chanting mantras. On one occasion, a light fluffy feeling moved through my forehead, and on another a tingling sensation moved through my scalp. Sometimes a burning sexual tickle moved through my prostate or up my spine. Each sensation filled me with bliss and happiness, giving me respite from my depression. I imagined that if I found a way to experience bliss forever then the little problems and questions of my life would matter little to me.

Death from a Vine

My brother was at it again. After our lengthy discussions about the nature of the spiritual path and the extreme depressions that came with it, he suggested that I try something new. He had some experience and knowledge in Shamanism and suggested that I try something that was known to help with depression. It was something called an Ayahuasca ceremony.

Ayahuasca was a vine grown in the Amazonian jungle. Shamans prepared this vine by mixing it with another plant and then boiling it in a certain way. I read a few books on it, and they revealed several accounts of miraculous healings of cancer and depression.

What else convinced me of Ayahuasca's validity was that most drinkers of the vine experienced extreme nausea and suffering. The plant was not a joy ride of any sort; it was definitely a medicine. On another note, in South America Ayahuasca was used in a number of rehab clinics.

Their success in using this medicine was nothing short of amazing. They claimed a rehabilitation rate much higher than the clinics in North America.

The other detail that sold me on Ayahuasca was that although a drinker of the medicine might go through hell during a ceremony, their life was experienced drastically different afterward. "More inner happiness," some said. There were also stories of men attaining Buddhahood by going into the jungle for several years to drink the medicine.

I decided to give it a shot. My depressions were brutal, and I wasn't going to infect the world with my misery. I was happier than I used to be, true, but that still didn't mean that my work on myself was finished. Arathi Ma had honored me by taking me this far, perhaps the medicine could speed along my spiritual evolution. Enlightenment and happiness were not options to me, but absolutes, and if I had to die trying to obtain them, then I was willing to do it.

And die I did.

My brother informed me that the ceremony was scheduled for Halloween weekend at a place somewhere on the Sunshine Coast. I was excited to go. So many of the stories I had read about the ceremonies included many amazing experiences. Bright colored visions, various physical sensations, loss of identity, purging of negative emotions, teachings that sometimes came in the form of spirits or alien beings were all part of the stories that I had heard. I focused on the good experiences, not the possible bad ones. Jamie's words came to me over and over, "It's either going to be the best experience of your life, or the worst."

Well, I should have seen what was coming when I caught the flu three days before the ceremony. My body ached and I was sure that a million miniscule construction workers had snuck inside my body to jackhammer my bones. I was also forced to partially close my left eye because it felt like someone had stuck an arrow in it. I didn't know how long it would be before the only word that came out of my mouth was "Arrrrrr" and the kids in the neighborhood resorted to calling me Jason the Pirate.

Arathi Ma made some chicken soup and brought it over to my Dog Mat. Indeed, life was grand. The kitchen was only five feet away, but I couldn't muster the strength to get up. I managed two mouthfuls of the soup, and then pushed it away. It seemed that Doggy had lost his appetite.

I rolled back and forth in perpetual motion and no matter how much Neo Citron I inhaled or drank, I received no respite from the pain. My hips killed me and my nose ran like slobber from a Bulldog.

I continued my mantras on the Dog Mat in silence and darkness (My sensitive eyes couldn't bear the glare from the television) and I have to admit that there was a hint of sarcasm in my voice when I rasped the mantras that had to do with healing. So far out of all the people that I knew, I had uttered more healing mantras by far, but yet there I was near death with a bowl of soup – closely resembling a dog dish – by my head.

Things got worse the next day. It was only one day until the ceremony, and I wasn't sure if drinking the medicine was the smartest thing to do at this point. After all, the shaman had sent out a list of dietary guidelines to follow and he was very strict about adherence to it. The list dictated that all medications and excessive sugar and salt were to be avoided. There were other guidelines as well, but I didn't have to worry about them because I wasn't eating much.

The medication part worried me a little because Neo Citron had been my poison of choice for the entire duration of the flu. The nagging voice in my head kept saying that if the goal of the ceremony was to induce a heart attack or a stroke the shaman's list would have said, "Step 1: contract the flu. Step 2: Drink a bucket load of Neo Citron or any other medication you can get a hold of. Step 3: Swallow plenty of salty liquids like chicken broth.

I had Arathi Ma double check the guidelines and we were pretty much sure that if I went to the ceremony, I'd either die or spontaneously blow up.

As the day etched on, I gathered the strength to call Jamie. I told him that I wasn't going to the ceremony.

"You're what?" Jamie said.

The judgment was clear in his voice. The note of "You're A Pussy" was strong in it.

"I can't go to the ceremony. I've had the flu and can't breathe very well. My chest is congested and I've had a _whackload_ of cold medicine that's contraindicated with Ayahuasca. The list that the shaman sent us is pretty clear that we're not supposed to use any medicines before the ceremony." I snuffled.

Jamie sighed, amazingly detached from the possibility of my death. "Oh, you'll be alright. Those are just guidelines."

Okay, now, that wasn't even fair. He was using his doctor title to convince me into taking the leap into the old blue yonder. I trusted my brother, but my trust was starting to dwindle. I made a mental note to scour his filing cabinets for an insurance policy on his brother the next time I visited his apartment.

"What? Guidelines? Are you kidding? Do you want me to die or something? These guys have been using this medicine for about twenty or so years and you think they sent us general guidelines? If there's no risk, then why did we have to sign a waiver?"

"That's standard stuff. Gyms have people sign waivers too. That doesn't mean that death is inevitable."

I blew my nose. "You're probably right, but I don't think that it's the best idea to try something that may require physical strength when I'm in this condition."

Jamie sighed. Things were clearly not going according to plan and he didn't like it one bit. He had told me how tortuous these ceremonies could be and he was not happy about going it alone.

Another thought also crept into my head. Since the dawn of time brothers have enjoyed causing some form of good-natured suffering to their siblings. I was sure that Jamie would have enjoyed seeing my massive ego get crushed. I admit that it could've used some crushing, but it wasn't my ego that I was worried about. It was dying. And I didn't mean it metaphorically.

A few days earlier, before the onslaught of the flu, I had been so sure of dying for my spiritual ideals. Now, as I stared my mortality in the face, I was no longer so sure about this dying thing. A little girly voice in the back of my mind taunted me, "Pansy boy, Pansy boy."

After another ten minutes of debate, my legs shaky with weakness, and Jamie disregarding my condition in totality, we decided that I wasn't going to the ceremony. I urged him to call me after it was done and let me know how it went.

I hung up the phone, guilt lingering around me like a bad fart. My brother was the best at a game I will call: Dirty Emotional War Tactics.

He had actually made me feel guilty for wanting to survive the next few days of my life. How did he do that? It was as if Jamie could shoot arrows of bad feelings in my direction and manipulate me into doing things that I had no business doing.

I talked to Arathi Ma about missing the ceremony, and she agreed with me. "We don't know what to expect, or how your system will react. I know you've been looking forward to the ceremony, but perhaps it's best if you do it some other time."

It was then, as she spoke, that a realization came over me. Arathi Ma had taught and given me so much. I knew that the waves of depression that came through me affected her life as much as my own. Of course she had the ability to transcend it; she could weather a million years of my depression and still smile through it all if she had too.

She was okay with it, but I was not.

I had an overwhelming feeling to serve her and I knew that I was incapable of it when depression overwhelmed me. I had a responsibility to her and to myself. My happiness would increase *our* happiness, so I renewed my resolve.

I decided that night that I had no other option. I was going to the ceremony.

The next day I rendezvoused with Jamie and another friend named, Greg. We hopped in Greg's car and took the twenty-minute ferry ride to the Sunshine Coast. The ceremony was another hour drive from the ferry dock so we'd be at our destination by approximately 5:00 pm.

The trip to the ceremony was short, but I still had plenty of time to think about what would happen to my meager possessions if I didn't survive the next two days. At least one positive thought came to me during the ride. Arathi Ma was very connected to the spirit world. So if God decided to stomp me out of existence, at least we could still communicate "long distance" so to speak.

Thoughts of my Arathi Ma brought a smile to my face, doing little to offset the green pallor of my skin, but brightening my mood nevertheless. Even when I wasn't around her, she was with me in spirit every step of the way. She knew that I was afraid of what was to come. I had heard many horror stories. It was common for people to get sick during the ceremony and such an experience could last six hours long. I couldn't imagine enduring a six-hour vomit fest after the hell I had already been through with the flu.

Jamie on the other hand, seemed all too happy to have his brother along. It seemed that Jamie could weather anything if his brother endured the torture with him. I asserted my concentration to a more positive direction. I had read that some people had claimed to see God during a ceremony. It sounded crazy, but even if seeing God was an impossibility, I longed to meet the majestic beings of light that Arathi Ma so often spoke of. She told me that masters of many kinds watched over us at all times, guiding us along our spiritual paths, guiding us home to a place of light and love. I had seen and experienced so many things around Arathi Ma, so I had no reason to doubt her words. Much of the energetic activity that I saw around her was probably evidence of such beings.

Greg pulled into the driveway of a large brown house. The house was located on the beach and was complete with a sweat lodge, heated dome, and several little beach cottages. Waves lapped against the rocky shore in gentle fashion and the scent of salt water welcomed us as we gathered our belongings from the trunk of the car.

We walked inside, organized our sleeping arrangements, and got settled in. Twenty people showed up for the ceremony so the sleeping quarters were a little cramped. Jamie and I were given one of the downstairs' bedrooms. I laughed out loud when I saw that the room obviously belonged to the owner's children who were out of town for the weekend. The bedroom contained three beds, two of them in bunk bed formation, and it reminded me of when Jamie and I were kids. When we were only six years old, I used to sleep on the bottom bunk and tell Jamie stories of monsters and magic while his eager feet dangled from above. They'd twitch with excitement or laughter when my story would hit a particular climax, or when it took a particularly silly turn.

This particular day, Jamie showed his true maturity by choosing the bottom bunk. I, on the other hand, had not reached that stage of development in my manhood; I was excited to sleep on the top bunk. I suppressed my urge for nostalgia when I spotted a spider on the ceiling.

I quelled my girl-like "Eek" and uttered a most manly swearword. I'm not sure if it appeared so manly though, because a shiver of disgust made its way through me and it must have appeared as if I was having a seizure.

Now, I don't know about you, but me and spiders have an understanding. If I and spider are walking down the street, I'll let the little guy go on his merry way. If I accidentally walk into his web and the little

guy gets on me, I'll brush him off in the most distinguished fashion --

albeit frantic – and go about my business. So as you can see, me and

spiders are just fine as long as they stay in their territory and I stay in

mine. Now if perchance a spider makes its way into my territory, I take it

as an act of war and it's kill or be killed.

I eyed the spider, telepathically communicating our territorial

agreement.

Jamie caught me eyeing the spider, smirked, and shook his head.

He had seen me in more than one physical altercation in my youth, so it

must have seemed absurd that a little spider could turn his brother into a

little schoolgirl.

That night we made our way to the large orange dome that was to

be the place for the ceremony. The dome was thirty feet across and was

complete with a fireplace. The floors were made of wood and it had a

most comfortable feeling to it. Everyone placed their sleeping bags and

foam mattresses against the wall, and pointed their feet towards the

middle of the circle. Everybody also had their barf buckets with them.

Some used paint buckets while others chose to bring old protein powder

jars. I used a small, old protein powder tub. My brother, on the other

hand, was prepared for war. A massive empty bucket sat on his lap. It was large enough for his arms to rest on the sides and it could have doubled as a toilet seat – maybe that was the idea because more than one person had crapped their pants during a ceremony.

The shaman sat across from us so that he was visible to everyone in the room. He was a small, white man and was well experienced with the medicine. I will not reveal his name because of the secrecy of the ceremonies, but I can say that he was one of the nicest, most humble men I had ever met. He took his work seriously, and sought the highest healing for everyone. This was more than a job to him; it was a way of life.

The shaman spoke. "Ayahuasca is a medicine with many teachings. It gives you the teaching you need at the time. You may want something specific, but it may give you something else instead. The Mother has her own wisdom and intelligence. She knows what is best for you."

In that moment, a giant spider made its way across the floor. Jamie sat to my left and on his left sat Greg. The spider scrabbled its way past Greg's blanket. Then moved past Jamie's blanket. The shaman still spoke, but I wasn't hearing any of his words.

The spider was heading my way!

Well, this was a clear violation of my Creepy Crawling Thing Territorial Agreement. One quick swat with my puke bucket was all it took. The loud clunk interrupted the shaman, and he was forced to clear his throat and continue.

Jamie chuckled and shook his head. His voice was a whisper, "Only my brother could kill something at a spiritual ceremony."

"What? It was going to get me. Did you see the size of it?"

The time came for us to drink the liquid. And due to the nature of the Halloween holiday, the shaman thought it would be funny to serve our Ayahuasca in a Halloween shot glass. When it was my turn to go to the shaman and drink, he chuckled and said, "Trick or Treat."

A treat it was not. The stuff tasted vile and good at the same time, as if someone had melted a bunch of old tires in a pot, threw in a few herbs, and then stirred until it came to life.

The lights were then turned off, the shaman lit a candle, and twenty of us sat in silence and meditation. Outside, only a hundred feet away from us, ocean waves crashed against the shore. Their constant rhythm dragged us deeper into relaxation. Ten minutes passed and the only thing I experienced besides relaxation was plenty of burping. The medicine seemed like it was having second thoughts about its journey into my tummy. I gave my stomach a few pats and it settled down for the moment. I then felt the brotherly eyes of cruelty upon me. Jamie seemed more excited about my experience than his own.

He smiled and said, "How you feeling?"

"Okay," I whispered.

So far.

Ten more minutes passed and then I started to see mist in the air. It darted this way and that, reminding me much of the phenomenon I saw around the apartment during Arathi Ma's meditations. The mist grew thicker and then the room started to move back and forth in the subtlest fashion. I started to feel a little seasick. I strategically placed my bucket in front of me and prostrated myself before of it. Jamie had told me what was to come, but there was nothing he could have said that could have prepared me for what came next.

The room started to rock. I thought that closing my eyes would help settle my vertigo. That was a mistake. As soon as I shut my eyes it was like HBO played inside my head and the brightest colors flew at me in all sorts of formations.

That was when the shaman started to play his music. A combination of drumming, rattling, and chanting. It was then that I learned the true power of sound.

The visions came in a more rapid, powerful manner. I saw all sorts of Halloween archetypes flying at me... and Batman and the Joker, although I cannot tell you what that meant.

My final vision was of a fly. I saw it close up in a most disgusting magnified way. A single thought came to me in that moment: Parasite, and then the vomit-fest began. I felt like the dog in the Movie "The Thing" and that something inside me was trying to turn me inside out. The sound of the most violent barfing I had ever heard engulfed the room, and I realized that the sounds came from me.

It continued faster and faster and it was so strong that I knew I was going to die. My brother's hand touched my leg and I heard him say something like, "Go with it. Don't fight it." I had no idea what he was talking about and I was too busy fighting for my life to find out. The visions came at me as bright as the sun, growing brighter every time I vomited into my bucket. I tasted blood and wondered if the small bucket that I brought was going to be large enough. My body went numb, sweat shot out from every pore in my body, and my heart thumped wildly in my chest.

Yup, I was dying; I was sure of it.

In that moment, Greg's laughter came to my ears. He and I had played hockey together, and due to the intensity of my competitiveness, he was enjoying my suffering tremendously. I thought then that if he only knew what was happening inside of me he would have found little humor in it.

One of the shaman's assistants rushed over the help me, and I heard myself say, "Jesus Christ help me, Shiva, Lakshmi, God." I didn't care which form of God showed up, as long as one of them did. In that moment if he showed up as a donkey, I would have bowed before him. I knew I must have done something to deserve such a fate and only God could help me now.

I can't remember the assistant's name, but he was the answer to my prayers. He was a tall, thin man, with receding hair and he emanated compassion.

His soothing voice came, "Let it flow, let it come up." I felt a hand on my back and it was filled with warmth. I struggled, swore, cried, and puked harder and harder. My nose ran like a river and I couldn't stop drooling in between bouts of nausea. If I wasn't crying on the outside, I definitely was on the inside. I tasted more blood, and I was sure that I had torn a muscle in my stomach.

"Let it move through," the assistant's voice came again.

It was then, in the crescendo of violence of sickness, in a place where I could suffer no further before death, that the light came. A light so beautiful and loving that I cannot express it properly in words. I collapsed forward onto my blanket, trembling as sweat poured down my face. If humility was a saintly attribute, I was God in that moment.

The light poured upon me, saving me from death, humbling me, filling me with overwhelming gratitude that such greatness would bless me with its presence. I didn't deserve its beauty, but there it was, blessing me, protecting me, overlooking my numerous flaws.

Golden gates appeared in the light and a smiling bearded man gazed at me from beyond. He appeared very majestic, as if he was a king of some sort. In the distance, the silhouettes of angels flew behind him. The gates blazed in the golden light and then there was a gentle pressure upon my shoulders, as if some blessing was bestowed upon me. The most comforting, warm sensation bathed my shoulders and neck, and it felt as if a cloak of rank and protection enveloped me.

I became immediately aware that the cloak was Arathi Ma's love. The blessing then moved its way through the rest of my body, filling me with its warmth and relaxation of an indescribable magnitude.

And then other teachings came.

The kingly man, who I believe was God in one of his or her various forms, faded away and I was shown several realms below his or her realm. Against the background of blue skies, a serpentine creature with the head of a woman and infinite tentacles stared at me in the most stoic manner. Her arms weaved the infinite, they moved in every direction making their way through all life. Tiny tentacles occupied her giant, blue, octopus-like arms and from them smaller and smaller appendages grew as well.

The shaman continued his chanting and I started to notice which music soothed my nausea and which music increased its intensity. When the nausea came I learned to allow the energy to flow upwards and doing so reduced my vomiting to the odd burp.

My visions directed me to another level downward and I saw a realm of green. I saw a Faerie being of some sort there. He was wearing a crown, showing that he was the reigning emperor of that realm and he looked like he was a hybrid between an elf and a goblin. Perhaps he was one of the elementals that Arathi Ma had told me about.

A collage of other visions came. They were of animals and shamans of all tribes. In that moment, I had a new reverence for the shamanic culture. Shamans were every bit the equal to all masters of various spiritual paths. I was humbled by the love that came from them and how they danced their way through the obstacles of life.

One particular shaman danced in my visions before me. He wore the pelts of a wolf, completing the outfit with a wolf head for a hat. He danced and danced, an ever-present smile upon his face. The wind blew wildly in his direction, and he only danced out of the way. He then turned and smiled at me, as if teaching me how to deal with the obstacles in my life.

The visions then transported me to the realm of light once more, and as I gazed at the beautiful heavens, golden words of scripture flew towards me. They grew larger and larger and ran into my forehead, almost as if I was downloading them into my mind. I tried to read the language, but couldn't understand it although some part of me knew that I had seen it before. The lines came, hundreds of them, the words blazing gold upon tan-brown paper. The words flared brighter as they grew closer and I was reminded of how the writing had appeared on the ring in the *Lord of the Rings* movie. The words kept coming and I wondered if they were the words of the divine and it frustrated me all the more that I could not understand what they meant.

Hours passed and the visions started to fade, as if a dimmer switch had been used to lower the amount of light in my mind. I then was left in darkness and extreme comfort with thoughts of love and gratitude for Arathi Ma flowing through every fiber of my being.

Her love had saved me from a brutal fate. I knew it. And I would never forget.

At 3:00 am my brother and I returned to our room. It seemed that our roommates, the spiders, were sleeping because they were nowhere in sight. The effects of the Ayahuasca had worn off, but even with my eyes open, I could sees more scripture flying towards me. I expressed it to Jamie and he shrugged, not understanding what it was or what it meant either.

In only minutes, after sharing some highlights of our experiences, we drifted into slumber. I cannot remember ever having a deeper more restful sleep.

I woke the next morning to see our room door open. The resident tabby cat, Abernathy, strolled in. He ignored Jamie and came straight to my bed. He jumped up onto my torso and purred, all the while kneading his paws into my chest. I got the sense that he was assisting with something.

He remained on my chest, working away for five minutes. Then when his work was finished, he sauntered out of our room. Feeling a little used, I guessed that he had more patients to see that day and had no time for chitchat.

I checked the time and it was 8:00 am. I'm not usually one to wake up at 8:00 am, especially after going to bed at 3:00, so I was surprised at how refreshed I felt. I eyed the ceiling for any spiders in search of an ambush and put on my pants and sweater. I strolled upstairs to receive the concerned stares from a few women that had attended the ceremony.

One blond girl in her mid-twenties tilted her head and gave me a concerned look, "How are you feeling today?"

There was genuine concern in her expression, but I felt somewhat judged by it. I'm sure that she wasn't judging me however, and I was more embarrassed about the severity of my experience than anything. My embarrassment made me extra sensitive when it came to anyone's commentary on how I had handled my first ceremony. That observation made me start to realize that I had to transcend my judgment of myself

A middle-aged lady caught my eye and said, "Boy, you really had a rough time last night, didn't you?"

I nodded, reddening somewhat, and I admit to a little bitterness about how easy everyone else's ceremony had seemed to go. My dying experience had been worth it of course, but I wondered if I had gone through hell because I was an awful human being, or if I deserved more suffering than everyone else.

Oh well, I thought, I would have gone through it a million times if it meant that I got to see that beautiful light again.

Feeling a little like the odd man out, I left the house and walked to the beach. I was amazed at what I saw and felt.

The air had a freshness that I hadn't noticed before. It seemed like every sense in my body had been retuned and heightened. I could taste the air, enjoy the presence of the sun on my skin, and actually feel the silky relaxation emitted from the sound of water gurgling over the rocky beach. It reminded me much of how I had perceived the world as a child. Somewhere along the way, adulthood had taken one sensation at a time from me until all that was left was the gray experience of numbness.

My spiritual work had slowly stripped away the numbness from my senses, but the ceremony had torn away another large layer of it. I was also sure that my mantra disciplines and the Ayahuasca had somehow worked together in a synergistic manner. I grew excited. I had experienced another miracle and could fully believe Arathi Ma's words, "Every experience is new -- no two are the same. Life – when truly experienced– is never boring."

I sat on a piece of driftwood staring at the waves. I felt vulnerable, wide open, and sensitive in a way that showed me that the walls of protection I had put around me – although useful in conflict – starved me of the experience of joy.

I sat for hours on that beach. The world and I were old acquaintances and finally after many years, we were reunited.

That night the second ceremony was held. The shaman told us that the medicine gave us what we needed at the time. Once it gave us the teaching, the medicine might not give any more teachings until the first teaching is integrated fully.

We drank and lay in the circle again. And although I prayed that the medicine wouldn't feel the need to kill me again, I decided that if dying was what I really needed, I would take the punishment with dignity.

Twenty minutes passed before I heard Jamie puke in his giant bucket and it sounded like a bad impression of a tuba. I decided that anyone seeking a silent meditation this night would get none of it with Jamie around.

Then it was Greg's turn. He vomited several times and then stopped for a minute before engaging in his own private hell. I thought about how he had laughed at me the night before and knew that the old me would have gotten pleasure from the poetic justice of it all, but I couldn't bring myself to even smile. I only remembered my experience and how I wouldn't wish it upon my worst enemy, let alone my friend.

The ceremony continued and I was surprised to find out that nausea eluded me. I didn't feel unsettled, dizzy, nor did I experience much of anything. Peace moved through me and I was free to watch the escapades around the room.

On one blanket, an older lady kept getting up off of her blanket and chanting to herself. It was a little creepy because I couldn't understand the language she was speaking. What made it worse was that as time wore on, she changed her language into that of a dog and her vicious barks echoed throughout the ceremony. She then got up and wandered about, causing one the shaman's helpers to have to "sit guard" in front of her to keep her from disturbing everyone.

I suddenly didn't feel too bad about how I had disturbed the ceremony the night before. It seemed that no one knew what would happen when it came to drinking the medicine.

Greg's sickness got worse and another helper rushed over the help him, but it seemed that poor Greg was getting no respite from his pain this night. The rest of the group responded to his wild reaction in much the same way, and the group that had been so calm during the first ceremony, came alive with the wild noises of nausea. It seemed that few people were impervious to the nauseating effects of the medicine this night.

I wondered if the extremity of it all had something to do with the fact that it was Halloween. I gazed into the darkness and I saw hundreds of misty ghosts flying this way and that. Perhaps the Halloween festivities had somehow engaged some other type of archetypal energy.

Things got weirder when we heard fireworks go off outside. The community was celebrating Halloween and it served as an interesting background noise to the shaman's chanting and the mayhem of nausea that grew in crescendo. I was reminded of seals at the circus playing various horns in elevating crescendo. Yes, it seemed, a masterpiece of some alien music was being created that night.

Jamie's tuba bucket. A young woman's metal plate. Greg's wild quick intense splatters peppering his small bucket in increasing frequency. Yes, we could have made Mozart proud.

The shaman's helpers ran about the room, answering the frequent "helps." Then in a surprising twist, one of the helpers, the man who had assisted me the night before, puked his guts out as he struggled to help Greg.

What a party!

If nausea was a sign of spiritual growth, at any moment I expected everyone to grow angel-wings and fly up to Heaven.

I sat in meditation, enjoying the silence within myself. Admiration bloomed inside me and spread to everyone at the ceremony. Each person searched for their divinity and was willing to go through hell to find it. I loved them all for that. Each had incredible courage and was willing to wage war on their demons so that they could truly connect to the world and I counted myself lucky to be among them on the journey. We were all the same. We all wanted more love. And in that night, the spiritual aspirants at that ceremony had it from me.

The Search for Truth

The next day, we said our good byes and were on our way home. There was something different in the firmness of the hugs that day. And there was an honesty and warmth in every conversation. Almost everyone had gone through some sort of emotional or physical misery and we were all closer because of it. I felt really connected to everyone, like their wellbeing mattered as much as or more than my own.

The ceremony had changed me forever.

Greg caught my attention and we made our way to the car with our stuff.

"Jason," he said, "Last night was brutal."

"Yeah, you must've processed some major stuff," I said. His mother had recently passed away, and I guessed that he had released some of his grief.

"Yeah, I did, but the worst part of it was that when I was in the middle of it all -- going through one of the hardest experiences of my life -- I expected you to laugh at me. And when you didn't, especially after I had laughed at you the night before, I felt like such a dick." Greg turned from putting his bags into the trunk, and gave me the biggest hug. "I'm sorry, man. I shouldn't have done that."

I was humbled by his apology. "Don't mention it. How could you know what I was going through?"

Greg, Jamie, and I drove to the ferry and had the most peaceful road trip any three guys had ever had since the invention of the car. I hardly spoke the entire way. I was too caught up in my new experience of life. Everything felt new to me, fresh, crisp, and bright.

So this was life, I thought. What it could be and I couldn't help but wonder how amazing it would be to experience the world through Arathi Ma's eyes.

A few hours later, I was home and sharing my experiences with Arathi Ma. I couldn't get them out fast enough. I told her about the first night of the ceremony and about how I had felt like I was going to die.

She nodded. "I sensed that at around 9:00 pm. I looked in on you and saw that you weren't doing so well. After I attuned to you everything seemed to settle down."

That must have been the cloak of warmth I had felt around my shoulders, I thought.

We ate dinner that night and overwhelming feelings of love and gratitude towards her came over me. She was such a normal person in so many ways, but she had been with me through the entire experience, keeping me safe, watching over me. She had magically connected with me during the ceremony and I had felt it, knew it with every fiber of my being. It seemed that there was no place I could go without the comfort of her soul beside me.

A few days passed and the clarity of my new realization started to fade. I remembered hearing the shaman say that the spirit of the medicine, the Mother, bonds with the drinker for quite a long time after it is ingested. The Mother continues to become one and heal the drinker for weeks or even months after the ceremony.

I didn't realize it at the time, but that was also an invitation for more spiritual cleansing.

Three days after the ceremony, a wave of depression hit me with such intensity it was all I could do to keep from throwing myself out of the apartment window. I could only compare it the feeling of losing a loved one: absolute grief.

The black fog of sorrow and depression hit me at about 7:00 pm and lasted until 10:00 that night. It was like one minute I was stuck in sorrow and then all of a sudden it left.

That was another moment that made me realize just how illusory my emotional states were. Time and again, I had been shown that my emotional state of wellbeing had absolutely no relationship to what was going on my life. I learned then, that if someone learned how to work with their emotional states, they could experience happiness all the time, no matter what type of drama was thrown at them.

Of course, a realization is one thing. Putting the realization into practice was another altogether. One didn't achieve this state of mastery over himself over night, but it sure as heck seemed worth pursuing. Any pursuit of happiness on the outside of oneself could be taken away, so that meant it wasn't permanent. I decided that finding happiness on the inside was the only permanent way to achieve it.

At that moment I decided that if happiness existed deep inside of me, then why couldn't I go get any job -- even if I didn't like it -- and turn it into a spiritual challenge. Happiness existed regardless of outside circumstances, right? I decided to test the theory. Besides, I had struggled with abundance most of my life because I had been looking for happiness through a perfect career or job. What if the type of job I had didn't matter? What if I could find fulfillment in any career?

I talked to Arathi Ma about it and she shrugged. "Your abundance is inside you. If you keep moving forward in your spiritual practice, eventually you will embody the very thing you seek. When that happens, abundance will come your way. Your expression for abundance will be your bliss."

She was speaking guru talk again, and although I sensed there was truth to it, I had a car payment coming up. She had taken care of the bills for the last few months and it didn't seem fair that I still had nothing financial to offer to our relationship.

"I've been doing nothing but abundance mantras and spiritual practice from day to night, and I haven't manifested anything financial yet. I know that spiritual disciplines aren't about money, but aren't they supposed to help someone find themselves in all aspects of their life?"

Arathi Ma smiled. "Not in the way you think. When someone is truly in their core, they do not worry about things in the same way. A spiritual master won't worry about how others judge them. They won't pursue money, status, or anything for that matter, if it doesn't come from their inner truth."

"Everyone has to eat, don't they?"

Arathi Ma tilted her head. "Yes, but some people need to do it in a nice house, or bring their groceries home in a car. A true yogi will live moment-to-moment, happy to sleep outside and eat when God produces their next meal. They aren't looking into how they can provide future meals."

"So they don't plan anything?"

More confusing guru talk. "Of course they plan. But only if their inner truth tells them to do so."

I was seeing a common thread though it all. "I think I understand. If someone is connecting to their inner truth, it could tell them anything, they only have to pay attention to it, right?"

She laughed. "Yes. When someone plans or uses their mind because of fears and attachments, they are stuck in the mind, stuck in thought. When that happens, they are not capable of *feeling* where their truth is or how it calls to them."

"Okay. So what's my inner truth telling me?"

She gave me a knowing smile. "Only you can know that."

I had no idea where my truth was, but one thought did pop into my head. I wanted to call an old friend. His name was Lee, and he managed a car dealership. I had some experience in sales and he had recently offered me a position.

I decided that working in sales would be a good temporary step for me. I couldn't see myself doing it forever, but all things led to something else, so I figured I'd give it a shot. "I'm going to call, Lee. I'm pretty sure that I can start work with him at the end of the month."

Arathi Ma hesitated and then nodded. "If that's what you feel your truth is telling you."

I shrugged. "I'm not sure if it's my truth, but I'll only learn by doing it and seeing what happens."

Arathi Ma nodded; she was a patient teacher and like she had done so often before, she instructed me on a yogic principle and then allowed me to struggle to find the deepest meaning of it.

I knew I was moving towards work because of the insecurity of being a man in his thirties without a job -- or an identity for that manner. The first question out of everyone's mouth when first meeting them was,

"What do you do?" It was embarrassing to tell them that I was in between jobs and dependent on my girlfriend for support. In other words, the sales job was not my inner truth. My inner truth told me to continue with my spiritual work, even *if* it didn't reveal abundance in the way I expected. My decision to work at the dealership wasn't really because I needed abundance. After all, Arathi Ma was doing okay with work and we were surviving just fine. My need for a job was more about *who* was bringing the abundance in.

To put it simply, I was taken care of. It was only my ego that wasn't.

I called Lee the next day and organized the details behind getting the job. I had to reapply for my salesperson license and that required a criminal record check. Once I was finished with all that, he said I could start work in a month.

I was a disappointed; I didn't want to wait another month. I was excited about going to work, about the possibility of abundance. I craved daily purpose and adventure. Not that a sales job held excitement and adventure for me. The only real exciting part was seeing how my spiritual disciplines manifested in the job. Would I experience more abundance than I had before in the same type of occupation? Or would I be happier with the day-to-day activities of a sales job?

The answers waited for me. All I had to do was start my job to find out. My entire life was a spiritual journey. After all, God worked through all things and I couldn't wait to see how he or she would manifest in the life of a car salesman.

I expressed my impatience to Arathi Ma. She weathered it, but seeing as I was a broken record of complaints about my finances, she finally got tired of it. I was in the middle of one of my tirades when she just got up and walked out of the room. I watched her go, my mouth still open as the words spilled out upon the floor.

I tried not to be offended and distracted myself by reciting mantras and watching television. A half hour passed and I heard the door squeak as Arathi Ma emerged from the bedroom. She wore a large smile and said, "I had a great meditation."

"Yeah," I said, smiling at the infectious nature of her good humor. "What happened?"

"Well, I know that your situation bothers you. I guess that was on my mind when I started to meditate. It wasn't long into my meditation before something happened. Ganapathi came. I asked him what we were going to do about your abundance problem and he answered me in the most stern manner, 'Oh Arathi," he said. 'Jason is worth more than you can imagine.'"

I had to laugh. I had seen Ganapathi once in meditation, but my awareness was not developed enough for actual communication. "He actually said that?"

Arathi Ma gave an enthusiastic nod. "He knows something. I don't know what it is, but he knows."

I felt much better after that. Spiritual truth was my highest aspiration, but I also knew that many years could pass before I attained it. I'd have to find my way in the world until then, and at least the message from Ganapathi gave me hope.

Arathi Ma, on the other hand, probably regretted giving me the message.

One day she returned home from work. I usually cooked dinner and cleaned up the kitchen as was the custom, but that particular day, I was behind schedule. I had gotten sidetracked with my spiritual practice and forgotten about dinner. Arathi Ma was starved and I felt bad that I had lost track of time. We started to prepare something together and I could tell that even though she hadn't voiced it, my forgetfulness had irritated her. Many things about Arathi Ma were *guru-ish*, but she still needed to eat like everyone else and I had agreed to make dinner after all.

It was clearly my fault. Despite the fact, I sought to dispel the tension. I grabbed her hand in the most romantic way, and gazed into her eyes with the most sorrowful look I could muster. "Oh Arathi, do not let this problem of hunger distract you from the truth. Don't you remember? 'Jason is worth more than you can imagine.'"

Arathi Ma laughed, and shook her head. Then her upbringing revealed itself in a barrage of Italian curse words flying my way. She followed them up with an exaggerated gesture of anger and then went back to preparing dinner, a smirk inching its way across her lips.

I then turned my head upwards and winked Ganapathi's way.

Patterns

My first day at work finally came, and I was introduced to the rest of the staff. My friend and boss, Lee, was from Hong Kong and had immigrated to Vancouver fifteen years earlier. He introduced me to a number of other employees that also emigrated from countries such as Singapore, South Africa, and China.

Each of them was well educated, but due to the bureaucracy of establishing their old careers in a new country, they chose a career in sales instead.

The dealership sold high quality import cars (I'll keep the type of import to myself for discretionary reasons). And Lee spent every moment chasing the next sale or following up with appointments. He was a workaholic. He was honest with everyone he met, and was educated on all matters when it came to his product. Any boss would have been lucky to have him.

Lee taught me the protocol involved in being a car salesman at the dealership. He showed me the showroom chair that clearly overlooked the car lot and informed me that when we saw a customer walk into the car lot, the sales personnel would take turns helping them.

The first day, it became clear to me that this was a rough place to make a living. Although salespeople received remuneration called a guarantee, it wasn't much more than minimum wage. We were mostly dependent upon the commission we generated from our sales. Of course, the more customers we saw, the higher chance of making a sale.

My shifts lasted six hours and most often I didn't see a single customer the entire time. I, of course, used the time as effectively as I could. I sat and performed my spiritual practice all day long by reciting my mantras over and over in my head

I often walked around with my mala (prayer beads) in my hand to keep track of my disciplines. This was a bad idea of course because it wasn't long before my coworkers referred to me as "The Buddhist" or the "The Monk."

I can't say I blame them. If my work with mantras hadn't produced so many amazing results, I would have thought that anyone chanting them was strange too.

As the days went by and the money was nowhere to be seen it became clear to me that I was at the dealership playing the role of a salesperson for other reasons than making money. No matter how hard I tried or how I sought to help my customers my sales didn't improve.

Bearing this in mind, I decided to focus onto my coworkers instead. I thought if I wasn't going to make much of a living, I might as well find a way to be of service to the people around me. After all, many gurus said that service was the most powerful karma buster. If I had bad money karma, then perhaps I'd have to "serve my way out of it." Besides, with only one or two customers a week to deal with, I had nothing but time. I spoke to my workmates for hours at a time, figured out what made them tick, and what made them happy. How did they see life?

I quickly realized that people contained a lot of patterns that didn't make sense. For instance, one workmate who I will call Ku, claimed that he worked long hours because his family was the most important thing to him. He'd work up to sixty hours a week and had high aspirations for his children to attend the best universities and acquire the highest stature in society. His yearly income, because of his indomitable work ethic in a tough economic environment, was approximately a hundred thousand dollars per year. He had established himself nicely even amidst the economic downturn in the automotive industry. After taxes, he'd have approximately five thousand dollars a month to support his family. Good right? That's what I thought until one Monday morning I found Ku dragging his feet while he paced around his office.

"What's wrong with you?" I asked. Ku usually immersed himself in his work. If there were no customers to serve, Ku was known to spend his entire day on the phone with his long list of regular clientele. Today, he was definitely not himself. His shoulders drooped and it seemed like something had drained the energy out of him.

"Nothing." Ku's Cantonese accent was thick and it was sometimes difficult to understand his words. He slumped into his chair and wiped his face with both hands in a dramatic fashion.

"Really, what's up?"

Ku made a frustrated sound. "Ah, I went to the casino on the weekend. I lost some money."

"Isn't that expected? I haven't been there much, but isn't that how those places work?"

Ku's head wobbled on his shoulders as if to express the stupidity of it all. "I lost forty grand."

"What? Forty grand?" I said. "Will you be okay?" I thought about Ku's family. What would they do for money?

Ku saw the concern in my expression and waved it off. "Don't worry about it. I have money in savings." He paused, shaking his head. "So frustrating. I work all the time and need a break once in a while. I go to the casino to rest my mind, get rid of my stress. I lose my shirt and get more stress instead."

I started to connect it together. "You go there often?"

Ku shrugged. "Once in a while. Once a week or every two weeks. I'm just frustrated 'cause I've lost money three weekends in a row."

I started doing the math. "That can't be good."

Ku's words came out in a most casual manner. "I lost a hundred grand. I'd have to work at this stupid place two years just to make it back."

A hundred grand! I couldn't believe it. Ku claimed to work hard so that he could give his family a great life, but here he was gambling away almost two years in wages in three weekends. There was no possible way he could sell enough cars to make up what he had lost. With income taxes being what they were in the higher tax brackets, he'd have to triple his wages to make his money back.

This pattern clearly didn't make sense according to what he had said about his highest values and ideals. Arathi Ma had told me that the mind and its compensations didn't make sense and this was as clear an indication of it that I had ever seen.

As the weeks rolled by, Ku lost more money. The odd weekend he'd be up, but then he'd lose everything again. He'd work longer hours, as if it would somehow make up for his loss, but the pattern never changed. His wife and children rarely saw him between his visits to the casino and his work, and yet he had said that they were his highest priority.

I counseled Ku often, but I don't think any of my words ever got through. He'd pretend to listen and then repeat the unsolvable problem of his losses all over again. He was so busy making up for what he had lost that he never thought about what he *had*.

I started to notice patterns in other coworkers as well. It was like the dealership was my Petri dish and my coworkers were a part of some ongoing study. I learned a lot about people, about how their fears and insecurities drove them. I also learned about how companies used these powerful motivators to influence consumers' decisions. It also became clear to me that most of our suffering came from clinging to a belief system or to certain way of life even if it wasn't working for us.

I knew that I had my belief systems too, but somehow they weren't obvious to me. I decided that it would take time for my awareness to grow, and to understand what beliefs were really mine and which ones had been imposed upon me by my upbringing in a materialistic society.

I continued to connect to my workmates, but I have to say, belief systems were pretty hard to crack. I had already decided that in Ku's case, I wasn't meant to help him, I was only meant to observe him.

Soon after I turned my attention to Hank, our used car manager. He was a well kempt Caucasian man in his mid forties. I didn't see eye to eye with him often, due to his acute ability to ignore the truth, even when it stared him in the face. Every day he showed up to work, and instead of doing what was needed, he deflected all attention away from himself by pointing out the flaws in everyone else. His work ethic was horrible and his knowledge of the product was even worse. He'd often disappear for hours at a time, to return and say he was at an auction or doing market research. Although this was true some of the time, most often he was on an extended lunch or shopping excursion.

Hank spent hours on the Internet researching which toy he would buy next, or gazing at pictures his band mates had posted on Facebook. It was clear that Hank did not enjoy his job and that he'd rather play music instead. His misery in his job caused him to spend money constantly and because his heart wasn't into his work, his earnings dwindled. Debt accumulated and he often complained about it. I wonder if he would have needed to accumulate all of his possessions if he had found a way to follow his passion for music.

I tried to point this out to him, but like most people, his patterns were too strong for him to break out of. He knew of no other way to live, and he wasn't in enough misery to want to break free from old habits.

I saw myself in him. Throughout my youth I had clung to an idea of success, of chasing a new idea or possession every moment of the day. This idea had come into my life and made me reduce every enjoyable moment to four miserable words, "I'll be happy when…" It seemed Hank had been caught in the same trap, and an insidious trap it was.

Still I used these four words from time to time, but when I caught myself using them, I knew that it was a sign that I wasn't seeing the "Now" for what it really was.

I shared my observations with Arathi Ma. She smiled at my ability to see the patterns in other people. I was, of course, mildly oblivious to the deeper patterns in myself, but she said noticing them in other people was a good step.

Observing my coworkers was fun, but when it came to the work, I was frustrated. Not only was I stuck in a workplace with little financial reward, I couldn't find a way of helping anyone either. No matter which workmate I tried to help, they clung to their miserable way of life like a drowning man to a floatation device. I learned that in many cases, patterns were the only sense of security and safety they had. The only pleasure they had ever known had come from what they already knew. Taking a leap into the unknown was too terrifying a step for most.

Arathi Ma came over to the chair where I was sitting and took her usual place by kneeling before me and resting her arms on my lap. Her eyes met mine, taking me deep into her soul. When she gazed at me like this, it was like my entire self could disappear into her. "Is it time for you leave?"

"I can't leave. If I do, I'm just falling for the 'I'll be happen when' trap. If I can't find happiness in anything, then I'm not spiritual enough yet."

Arathi Ma tilted her head. "Being spiritual doesn't mean you have to martyr yourself. If you leave, you are doing so because you're using discernment."

I guffawed. "What am I going to do then? Leave everything when it gets too hard or difficult."

Arathi Ma's gaze was intense. "Is the beauty of life supposed to be pain and suffering to you? Life is a dance, a love-making, not a war. You have a choice as to which it will be for you."

I guess it was akin to saying that you always got what you looked for.

"How do I know when I'm just avoiding responsibility or being lazy?" I said.

Arathi Ma was hunting belief systems again. "If you are standing in a fire, and it causes you incredible agony, are you lazy if you decide to step out of it?"

I shook my head. "Of course not."

"Then why is it any different when you try to make yourself do something that doesn't fulfill you? Every soul has her own special gift to share with the world and each has its special way of doing it. If selling cars is not how your soul wants to manifest in this world, is that wrong?"

I understood her, but that didn't solve the problem of *how* I was going to manifest a living. I sighed. "What do I do now then?"

"Continue your spiritual practice. Your gifts will unfold in time."

Gifts? So far, I hadn't been able to help anyone. I was regarded as a nut-ball that chanted mantras all day and night. If I had any gifts, they were nowhere in sight yet.

"I wish these so called gifts would show up"—I turned my face upwards to the ceiling –"Hello? Gifts? Come on! Time to show up now. I'm kinda sick of waiting for you."

Arathi Ma slumped her head on my lap and her words came out muffled. "You're crazy."

If I quit my job, I knew that I'd have to face a whole smattering of guffaws of disappointment from my parents and my brother. Jamie seemed happiest with me when I was "sucking it up" and suffering like everyone else in a job that I hated. I think he saw it as a worthwhile punishment for not getting an education like he had suggested.

Jamie enjoyed his work, and had encouraged me to start school so that I could go into the direction he had chosen. He chalked up my lack of enthusiasm for school as laziness, but that was only partially true. I just couldn't see myself pouring four to eight years in the pursuit of something that I didn't want. I wanted passion in my life, not a career for the sake of a career.

Jamie had various rules and reasons why my expectations were unreasonable in the way I chose to pursue them, but I ignored them. These rules were right for him, and had worked very well, but they did not resonate with me.

The moment I thought of quitting, yet another job, I started to wonder if Jamie had been right all along. Perhaps I had just taken the easy way out. This disagreement between us had gone on for as long as I could remember, and so far, it appeared as if Jamie was winning the "Race of Life" by a landslide. If I died that day, I could imagine what would be written on my tombstone. "He should have gone to school."

Who knows? Maybe Jamie was right.

This all passed through my thoughts when Arathi Ma asked, "Are you going to quit?"

I caught her gaze and shook my head. "I can't quit. Not yet." I knew it was coming, but if I stuck it out a little while longer, maybe things would turn around.

Arathi Ma sighed and said, "Okay, remember your truth. It doesn't depend on what others think, or the glorification of the ego. Those things don't matter to your soul. Catering to the ego stifles the soul, keeps it from giving you true happiness."

I contemplated her words. They sounded right, but I could not think of a way to make them work in my life. I decided that more mantra and meditation were necessary for me to fully understand, so I did what I most often did with her profound statements – I let her words sink in. In the future sometime, the "aha" moment would come.

I continued to go to work during the day, and perform my spiritual practice at work and at night. My meditations had gotten deeper, so deep in fact that it was a common occurrence to blank out altogether for an hour at a time. I'd wake up suddenly almost like I had been teleported away to reappear back in my body. I'd then collapse sideways and go to sleep on my Dog Mat.

On another occasion, I decided to meditate in a chair. I turned off all of the lights and only the smallest hint of a glow from the streetlights crept in through the glass balcony door. I sank deeper and deeper into meditation. The sensation of energy grew stronger and hummed through my limbs and torso.

There was a sudden crash behind me and I shot up out of my chair. My heart thumped wildly in my chest and I jumped up to flick on the lights. It was then that I saw what had caused the commotion. The vent above the stove had fallen off and crashed onto one of the elements. I could not figure out how it had happened. The entire six months Arathi Ma and I had lived in the apartment, the vent had never fallen off. Had the energy created from the meditation caused it? I couldn't be sure, but I knew one thing for certain, my meditation for that night was finished.

Arathi Ma had told me once, that spiritual experiences were infinite in variety. So far I had experienced visions, bliss, physical sensations of various types, prophetic dreams, and now I had experienced something physical.

And the experiences continued.

Another night I was in deep meditation and saw an East Indian teenage boy. I couldn't figure out for the life of me who the boy was. I had never seen him before in a picture or movie of any sort. Months later the answer came to me. I had been working with the Markandeya Mantra for quite some time when I came across a teaching by Namadeva in one of his books. He said that it was common for the immortal teenager, Markandeya, to visit those that chanted his mantra. Although I cannot know for sure, I have a strong suspicion that my vision was of him.

I was thankful for my spiritual experiences. They gave me respite from the boredom of my work. They got me through the day, and helped me weather the grumpiness that hung around me like a cloud. I was also thankful that I had Arathi Ma to share my experiences with. She listened to my stories with as much enthusiasm as my own and added her thoughts on what had happened and where it had also happened to her on her spiritual path. It was a gift to have her in my life. I was aware that many other spiritual seekers had no one to share their experiences with and when they did, their stories would be met with ridicule, or a polite "that's nice."

The spiritual path had taught me much about people. One of the most illogical things that I learned was that if someone hadn't had the same experience as you, your experience was somehow discredited.

I hope that this book serves as your own "Arathi Ma" on your road to enlightenment.

Who Am I?

A month had passed since Arathi Ma and I had our conversation about leaving my job. I admit it; selling cars was driving me crazy. Not only did I have to endure the conflict between coworkers as their contradictory belief systems collided, but I had to endure the customers as well. No matter how hard I tried to connect with people on a personal level, they saw me as a salesperson first and foremost. In their minds a salesperson was someone to be wary of and due to some of the unruly sales tactics I had seen, I couldn't say that I blamed them.

The fact remained that I wasn't much of a salesperson. My focus wasn't on selling, but on connecting. The sales business wasn't for me. I was a straightforward kind of guy, and the customer's constant second-guessing of my motives was toxic to me.

When I received an email stating that there would be another Ayahuasca ceremony, I leapt at the opportunity. I hoped to discard any other patterns that were hindering my evolution, and I prayed to connect with the light that I had seen in my first experience. I wondered what the medicine would teach me this time around.

The ceremony was in Chilliwack, an hour away from where I lived. A small hobby farm served as the host, complete with a metal swing gate that opened to reveal a long dirt driveway. I arrived to the property at sunset, my car headlights catching several pairs of glowing eyes. Howls of greeting came and I noticed that the eyes belonged to the three dogs that patrolled the property. They came in brown and yellow tints and appeared to have a little Retriever in their bloodlines. I loved dogs, so when I got out of the car I expected one of them to come over for a pat or two. I was surprised to find that as soon as I moved towards any of them, they shot off into the yard under the cover of darkness. Their behavior reminded me much of wolves, but I'm not sure why. They were much smaller than wolves, and weren't intimidating in any way, but there was something about their behavior that reminded me of a pack mentality. These dogs were definitely a unit.

Always aware that teachings from the divine came from everything, I wondered what teaching the dogs had brought to me.

I walked into the house and Meredith, the host, directed me downstairs. The ceremony was to be held in a large empty basement. It was comfortable. Light came from various candles and the floor was carpeted so it was easy on the back to lie upon. I laid out my blanket, placed my bucket in front of me, and saved a spot beside me for my brother, Jamie. It wasn't long before he arrived, and we glanced at each other more than once when it came time to drink the medicine again. We both revered the medicine with nervous respect. It gave the drinker what they needed, but the irony is that everyone needed a good shit-kicking from time to time. No one ever knew which night theirs would come.

I was glad to see the same shaman that had performed my first ceremony. He was a small, jovial kind of guy, and he was always good for a laugh. I knelt before him and bowed to show my respect for his work. He bowed in turn and poured a shot of the reddish-brown liquid.

The shaman smiled, and said, "Bottoms up."

I drank the concoction and I was surprised to notice that the stuff actually tasted worse. The shaman saw how my face scrunched up under the taste of rubber and herbs, and said, "Good stuff. The more you drink, the worse the taste gets."

I nearly vomited right then and there. I lumbered back to my blanket, belching a portion of the medicine back up into my throat. I grimaced when Jamie caught my eye. I shook my head; I was starting to wonder if God was worth this much trouble.

The medicine kicked in about thirty minutes later and the nausea came. I didn't vomit though. I would get the feeling of nausea and then it was almost as if the plant was teaching me how to open the chakras in my throat and stomach. As soon as I relaxed those areas, the nausea faded for a few minutes before returning to teach me how to open up those areas again.

I had struggled with heartburn for several years, but the first ceremony I had attended on the Sunshine Coast had healed a large portion of it. This ceremony, it seemed, was continuing the work on my digestive system. Burning sensations would emerge from my stomach and travel upwards and when I was forced to belch, the air was hot and warm.

The next night, Jamie decided that he had gotten all the teachings that he needed. I encouraged him to stay, and I'm sure that the panic of not having my brother beside me in case I had a bad experience was evident in the fluttering of my words. He refused to stay and said that he would offer some prayers for my protection. He then wished me luck and went home.

That night, the ceremony was more of the same. I drank, sat down, and waited for my reality to shift, or to have an overpowering experience. I couldn't help but grieve the absence of my brother and to be truthful my grief wasn't altruistic. If the medicine decided to give me a heart attack or put me into some coma, it was handy to have a doctor nearby. Of course my fears were unfounded; after all, the medicine healed people, it didn't kill them. At least, not literally.

Soon enough, the effects of the medicine kicked in. I didn't die, didn't see God, didn't see creatures or beings of ambiguous origin; I only had the sensation of warmth leaving my stomach. I didn't vomit often, but when I did, it was filled with heat, acid, and the taste of the medicine. The medicine was working its healing magic on my digestive system and I applauded its efforts. In my daily life, I was sick of watching every little thing I ate in an attempt to avoid heartburn.

I was also aware that the third chakra (right in front of the stomach) was where we stored a lot of our karma. I had a sneaky suspicion that my heartburn was caused or at least aggravated from an extreme state of spiritual cleansing. My spiritual practice was elaborate and intense, which stirred up all sorts of emotional patterns that then worked their way through my energetic system. The pace of this, of course, was sped up from the presence of Arathi Ma twenty-four hours a day. She was like a nuclear power plant of spiritual energy.

The final night of the Ayahuasca ceremony came, and although I was pleased that the medicine had chosen to work on my physical body the first two nights, I was disappointed with the lack of spiritual phenomena. I craved for the light to return to me, to see the Kingly face of the God I had seen before. I have to admit that my mind always held onto doubt, despite all the mystical things I had experienced. The spiritual experiences helped me hang onto my faith in my pursuit of God. They were my breadcrumbs leading me forward. Without them, I feared that my ever-doubting mind would destroy my spiritual quest and that my faith would somehow dwindle underneath it.

I expressed this to the shaman. "I haven't had any visions or teachings that I can decipher. Why isn't the medicine working?"

The shaman smirked, as was often his expression. "You want visions?"

"I don't have to have them, but it's nice to have an experience other than puking my guts out."

The shaman nodded and repeated his mantra. "The medicine gives you what you need. I studied with the medicine for years before I saw anything. It's fun seeing the light in ourselves, but it is not so fun to experience our own darkness. You can't move forward until you learn to accept the darkness."

I wondered what the shaman's experience of the ceremony was. "Are your visions strong?"

"Let's just say this, when the visions do come, they come so strongly that you cannot get away from them. Open eyes or not."

The shaman poured the medicine for me and I drank one last time. I couldn't help but notice that he poured a little larger dose this time around.

I went and sat on my blanket, the disappointment of my last two nights' still strong in my mind.

Another night, I thought.

Get sick, feel like crap, and then go home. I decided that this would probably be my last ceremony. Perhaps the medicine was done teaching me.

I sat for a long time on my blanket in meditation. I felt good. No nausea. No burning. No sensations out of the ordinary. Perhaps I had mastered some part of the medicine.

I'm not sure how long I clung to the ghost of that thought before it was shattered.

I suddenly heard some commotion outside the window. The dogs were going crazy about something and they were barking and howling as if they were on the hunt. I then heard the roar of a black bear. It was distinct and real. It wasn't a trick of my imagination; it was a real as anything I had ever heard. It was also altogether likely because bears were known to roam the woods in the farm's area.

A few minutes after the bear's roar something really strange happened. The room started to shift before me, almost turn on its side. I then lost all sensation of the left side of my face before it fell away from me, and I wasn't sure if I was having a stroke. I confess to a little fear in that moment, but there wasn't anything I could do to prevent the process.

Then I opened my eyes to get my bearings and saw the floor swirling with movement. It was like white snakes writhed all over the place. Nausea came and I collapsed forward onto my bucket and hung on for dear life.

Oh God! Here we go again.

I apologized for ever wanting a vision at that point. I kept repeating, "I take it back, I take it back." But it seemed that no one was listening. A barrage of visions came to me. Wolf heads floated before my eyes, but what made them strange was the fact that they had purple tentacles reaching out in every direction. The tentacles grossed me out and I struggled to push the pictures away, but when I opened my eyes my nausea grew worse because of the moving floor.

The shaman's music played faster and faster, increasing the intensity of the experience. Actually, increasing the intensity doesn't properly describe what the music was doing.

It was pissing the medicine off!

The dirtiest emotional sensations moved through me as the colorful visions passed before my eyes. Shame, guilt, boredom to an extreme that I had never felt before moved through me, and I could not imagine where such emotions came from.

The visions suddenly changed from animals to a small medieval village. People screamed and ran in every direction, their hovels in flames behind them. Livestock scattered about and I stood among pigs and villagers under a hail of long spears. Blood and gore ran under foot and people were slaughtered with the same indifference as the animals. I had the sense that I was a girl and I felt totally helpless amidst the mayhem.

The movie projection in my mind shifted. I was on a battlefield. Fresh corpses beyond count lay before me, adding intensity to my nausea I never thought possible. I shut my eyes as strongly as I could in a pitiful attempt to block out the gore of it all, but there was no hiding from it. Sometime, somewhere, I had seen all of it before and I still carried that energy with me.

Past life, I thought.

The pictures changed again, so rapidly that I cannot remember all of them, but what happened next was the scariest of it all. A city appeared before me. I was amidst tall buildings of orange and green and the colors were so bright they could have passed as cartoons. And in that moment, amongst those buildings, I forgot who I was.

I didn't know where I was.

Why I was there.

Or what I was supposed to be feeling. I had no knowledge of myself whatsoever. I had no idea that I was Jason, a man who had decided to partake in a ceremony. I became pure awareness with no identity and the fear of it was surprising. I had nothing to anchor onto.

I snapped out of it, and found myself in the midst of the cartoon village. The nausea came in a stronger wave, as if the process of forgetting myself released some greater part of my identity that was no longer useful. My sickness grew uncontrollable at that point and one word came out of my mouth in a groan, "Help."

In a moment the shaman was there playing his music, this time soothing in nature. My insides immediately calmed and in that moment, I loved that man more than I had ever loved anyone. He was my lifeline. My savior.

I thought, thank you. A million thank-you's to you, and a million more to your mother for giving birth to you.

Realization and a Dream Initiation

The next day I called Jamie and started to share what had happened on the third night of the ceremony. I said, "I drank the medicine and waited for something to happen. It took quite a while and the weirdest thing was that I heard a bear's roar before the medicine even kicked in. And--" Jamie cut me off right there.

"A bear. How do you know it was a bear?"

"The roar reminded me of the sounds that came from the bear documentaries I've seen. The sound was definitely bear-like."

There was a chuckle on the other end of the phone.

"What's so funny?" I asked.

"I told you I'd pray for you, didn't I? I sent you a spirit animal as an experiment. Guess which animal I sent to protect you."

"A bear?" I said, the words falling out of my mouth in awe.

The strange part was that this wasn't the first time this had happened at an Ayahuasca ceremony. Jamie was the first of the two of us to partake in the ceremonies and the first time he had gone, I was doing my own experimentation with animal meditations. At that time I had practiced shamanic meditations for almost a year, and due to the intensity and colorful activity of my dreams, I was sure that something magical was being invoked from the practices. Jamie asked me to wish him luck because he had no idea what to expect from his first ceremony and I decided to use his experience as an experiment instead. Did the medicine really tap into truth? Or were all the visions in someone's head? And, was I really invoking the energy of animals when I meditated upon them?

That night, I sat down and meditated upon the scariest land animal I could think of: a crocodile. I asked the animal to protect my brother during the ceremony. The next day when he shared his experience with me, he told me that the first thing he saw was the image of a crocodile.

Hard to believe, but it happened.

It proved to me that there was truth to both my meditation practices and the Ayahuasca ceremonies.

The next day I went to work and I admit that the coming week was an emotional challenge for me. The ceremony had freed something deep inside me, I knew, but it was not a painless process in letting it go. This experience had been nothing like the first ceremony I had attended. Whereas the first ceremony had left me full of life, and given me a brighter more wondrous experience of the world, this group of ceremonies left me with overwhelming feelings of boredom and dullness. Shame and guilt were also emotions in the mix, but there were so many dark feelings that I don't know where one began and the other one ended.

One day I arrived home with boredom beyond description flowing through my entire being. I had never heard of someone dying of boredom, but that day, I really believed that it was possible. I decided that my sales job was the cause of my boredom. Constantly waiting for customers that never showed up was hard on the morale. It wasn't unusual for me to go to work, take three phone calls, go to lunch, and then return to finish my shift without a single interaction.

I hung up my coat, changed out of my dress pants and shirt, and went to the living room and collapsed onto the Dog Mat. Arathi Ma emerged from her room and came over to greet me. She halted when she saw my face. "Have a bad day? You don't look so happy."

She knew what I was feeling, she was too in tune to not know, but I indulged her for conversation purposes. "Bored. I've been bored lots of times, but never this bored. How can Boredom get more intense? I didn't think Boredom was something capable of intensifying. You never hear someone say, 'Wow, what an intense experience of boredom, do you?'"

Arathi Ma smiled. "It'll pass."

"Pass? How can boredom pass? Isn't boredom a side effect of the crappiness of my life? My job sucks; that's why I'm bored. The boredom is real. "

Arathi Ma kept her smile. "Is it? Were you this bored last week when you were performing the same job, doing the same thing?"

I thought about that for moment. Last week had been as slow as this one. Was probably even slower, but my mood last week was measurably better. I came up with a reason. "Last week I was looking forward to the ceremony. Maybe that helped keep the boredom away."

"So you're saying that thinking differently changed your experience of life? The ceremony was in the future so you changed your attitude in the moment because of another thought."

"Yes," I agreed.

"So if you can change the way you feel in any moment with a thought, is the original feeling real? Or even necessary? Anything that can be discarded that easily, isn't coming from your core."

Then the lights in my head went on. I leapt off the Dog Mat in excitement. So far on my spiritual path, I had realized the phenomena of spiritual cleansing. I knew that it was possible to experience extreme bouts of anger, depression, anxiety, irritation, or sadness when I was cleansing them from the psyche, but I had never imagined that I could cleanse something else as well: boredom.

"So, I'm cleansing the experience of boredom." I smiled with satisfaction in the realization.

Arathi Ma laughed and clapped her hands. "Good, you got it."

"And when I discard the boredom, what lies underneath is closer to my truth, right?"

She nodded. "Nothing on the outside is real. It is utterly dependent on perspective. Learn to discard painful perspectives and the outside becomes joy and bliss. The state of the true self is nothing but joy and bliss, so anything other than that is an illusion created by the mind. That is what enlightenment is about."

The boredom suddenly became bearable; I knew it would pass. I wondered then that if other people knew, truly knew, that enlightenment was about removing emotional pain from their lives, if they would be so quick to reject the common practices used in the pursuit of it.

Removal from emotional pain was what everyone wanted. I knew that. Convincing them that it was possible was the difficulty. I was lucky to have Arathi Ma to show me.

Through her teachings, yet again, I had made another major realization.

It seemed the universe was always watching. It wasn't long before I had a magical dream. In the dream I watched a scenario unfold, as if I was watching television. A black man with Rastafarian hair was surrounded by men and women who bowed at his feet. There was an obvious shroud of power around this man, and although he was revered by the people around him, I got the sense he wasn't one to be trifled with. I wondered who this man was. Was he a guru?

Not liking the fear that I had of this man, I tested my courage by throwing energy in his direction. It was like throwing my soul towards him to probe for information.

The man immediately reacted by running towards me. He grabbed me by the shoulders and my body went limp in his grasp. "Who are you?" he yelled.

My answer came out weak, as he had somehow paralyzed my body. "My name is Jason. I only wanted to know if you're a true guru." I was well aware of the gurus that misused their power, and I wondered if this man was one of them.

As in answer to my concerns, the guru pointed at me, and then everything went black. I was blind. I still was aware of the man before me, so I pleaded my case. "I didn't mean any harm. I only wanted to know who you were."

There was a word uttered in a language I didn't understand and my sight returned.

The spiritual master stood before me. "What is your lineage?" he asked.

"I don't have one," I said.

"My lineage comes from master…" He mentioned a name here, but I did not recognize it. He asked me if I knew of several other masters and I said that I had no knowledge of them.

The master sighed, as if dealing with a child in adult matters. "You do not know these great ones? How could you not?"

I realized then that we were in a small room with wooden floors. Ten feet in front of me was a platform that sat one foot off the ground. The master walked up onto the platform and turned to face me. "Sit," he commanded.

Not wanting to be blinded again, and knowing that I was in the presence of true power, I obeyed. The master then gestured to some men sitting off to the side of the room. They started to beat their large drums in a ceremonial sort of way while the master performed various postures before me. In one such posture, he put the heel of his foot into his mouth. Powerful energy spewed forth from him and radiated into my forehead. The energy was strong enough to nearly knock me flat onto my back. This was a true master indeed.

My forehead started to vibrate with a deep pulsing hum, and I knew that I had just received an initiation of immense power.

I woke up with a start. I was on the Dog Mat, my face crinkled up onto my pillow. I glanced around the room, searching for a sign of the master. The dream had seemed so real. I felt my forehead and it still buzzed with the amazing energy the master had blasted into me. Seeing no sign of the master's visitation, but feeling the presence of great energy, I decided to ask Arathi Ma if she knew what had happened.

I pushed open the door to her room and said, "Something amazing just happened. I think I just met a master."

Arathi Ma pointed. "Yeah, you did. He gave you an initiation. I can feel the energy pulsing in your forehead."

A Guru's Work

I had learned so much by observing Arathi Ma, but most of the things I learned were not obvious at first. For instance, for a long time I had watched Arathi Ma run workshops and meditations and it was common for her to initiate students into certain energies or spiritual practices. I remember that when she had given me my initiations I had thought that it was easy for her and that the entire process was nothing more than her wielding her magical ability with little or no effort.

As workshop after workshop came and went, I noticed that there was a predictable pattern to her mood in the days after giving such initiations. If several students brought grief to the workshop, Arathi Ma's mood contained a tinge of grief in the days after. If students brought physical pain, then Arathi Ma carried that as well after giving them an initiation. I soon realized that it didn't matter what emotional burden or ailment a student had, Arathi Ma would take on all or some portion of it in the days after.

Many times she complained of a sudden physical ailment in the form of a question. "My back hurts, I wonder how that happened?" or "I feel sick, was it something I ate?" And she was always quick to feign surprise when I pointed out the student that had complained of the same physical affliction as her own. In a stroke of coincidence, that student would also mention that his or her ailment had suddenly left or lessened to a large degree after receiving an initiation from Arathi Ma. If I was her, I would have used the opportunity to explain to the student how I had taken the burden from them, but Arathi Ma wasn't concerned with such things. She only smiled at the students' mentioning of miraculous healings and then offered some other advice to keep their problems from reemerging.

I came to know, that even though Arathi Ma suffered with the various patterns of her students, the difference between her and them was that she was capable of flowing the condition through her. In a few days of suffering, she could flow a pattern of sadness or despair, when the student might have spent an entire lifetime on it. I asked her about the process a few times and one day she decided to answer. "My students don't know that they are something other than their pain. I know that I am not the pain, so I can move it through me whereas they cannot. This takes them closer to realizing that they are not their suffering so that it becomes possible for them to awaken. I guess you can say that I remind them of who they are. When they are reminded enough, they will have deeper and deeper realizations, and then one day their suffering will stop."

"Is there a way to initiate them without suffering yourself?"

"I don't suffer in the way they do, but I still feel their stuff. So I guess the answer is yes and no. Perhaps when I evolve more, the process will change." I knew that she was speaking of Nirvikalpa Samadhi. It was the final dissolution state of a spiritual seeker before they made it to full enlightenment. Although she had not experienced this state yet, she felt that it was near.

I wished that there was a way for Arathi Ma to initiate people without having to take on the patterns of the students. Often Arathi Ma would suffer the patterns of her students after her workshops, but it was not uncommon for her to have similar experiences the night before giving initiations too.

I remember many instances where her mood would suddenly shift the night before a workshop. She'd be her happy normal self, and then a wave of grief would move through her. Sometimes the extremity of it would cause her to cry, and I'd be incapable of easing it in any way because the grief had no origin. The only thing I could do was offer my own energy in the form of healing in order for the pattern to move through her faster. In only minutes the "cleanse" would be finished, and Arathi Ma was her normal innocent self again. And sure enough, the next day it would just so happen that one or several of her students were grieving some major part of their lives at the time. I don't know why this happened on some occasions rather than others. Perhaps her soul made the decisions on when or how to give each initiation. Maybe it was less of a burden to cleanse the patterns of her students in chunks rather than flow all of them at once.

It is important to note, that most people would not have observed this behavior on the level that I did. I had absolute faith in what was going on because Arathi Ma had proven her power to me over and over again. Many observing this type of behavior, who didn't understand who Arathi Ma was, condemned her for it even though she was doing the highest service for those initiated. When it was time for Arathi Ma to move an emotional pattern through her, their simple minds would say "That doesn't make sense to me" or "Why does she need to meditate right now? It's an awfully inconvenient time" and so forth. They couldn't understand the complexity of her work. Most people worked within their five senses, Arathi Ma did not. She had a whole other list of senses to work with, coordinate, and respond to. And although I appreciated all that she had done for me, I was also aware that much of it had eluded my limited awareness.

A Great Man

Soon came time for when my brother, Jamie, brought Namadeva to our hometown to teach a workshop on mantra, Puja ceremonies, and their origins. I had read many of Namadeva's teachings and was eager to confirm the great things I had heard about him. Arathi Ma indulged my enthusiasm by joining me.

The workshop was held in a little community hall, complete with a pool table, mini kitchen, and community bookshelves filled with videos, DVD's, and novels. Jamie and his partner, Tara, had placed twenty chairs in a semicircle and Namadeva sat in the center to play his Tambura.

Namadeva was a Caucasian man in his sixties. He was bald and there was little meat to his bones, but the way he looked wasn't his most notable characteristic; it was how he made you feel. A beautiful energy came from him and I had the overwhelming urge to give him a hug. I expressed this to him at some time during the workshop and he gave me the warmest smile and said, "I hear that a lot." Then without another word, and a twinkle in his eye, he went and sat in his chair to instruct the group.

Namadeva's teachings were accurate and abundant. He had practiced mantra and Vedic Ceremony for forty years and anyone who spoke to him would readily agree that he was indeed the North American expert on the subject. He had a way of teaching that was so gentle and compassionate.

One student asked, "I can't pronounce these mantras right? Will they still work for me?"

Namadeva returned, "Does a mother love her child any less when it tries to babble its first words?"

He also taught of gurus, how there were different kinds all working towards the same end. Some were filled with humility and compassion, and eased suffering everywhere they went, while other gurus *created* misery and suffering in order to shatter the illusions of the ego. Namadeva was also quick to say that these same gurus would only cause harm to the ego while protecting the divinity in their students at the same time. No *true* harm was ever done by any type of guru, but some were more aggressive than others in doing their work. I wondered what "true harm" looked like. After all, Namadeva also said that if one was lucky enough to be killed by an Avatar (incarnation of God) they were instantly liberated from rebirth.

Namadeva also told stories of what it was like to be in the presence of a guru. I found this terribly ironic because he was a guru, but he never gave any credit to himself in that capacity; he only spoke of the greatness of others. In one story, he spoke of his late Guru Sant Keshavadas. The strength of this guru's energy was such that Namadeva said that although he was always excited to see him, in as little as three days, he couldn't wait for his guru to leave. Namadeva made a twitching movement with his eyes, like he was being electrocuted and mimed a shooing motion. I knew that Namadeva spoke of the powerful spiritual cleansing that would follow a visitation of a guru. All sorts of controversy would join such a visit as everyone's emotional patterns got dredged to the surface.

I doubt that many truly understood what that actually looked like.

I did.

Namadeva also said it was common for conflict and controversy to surround gurus.

I knew the reason for this. Gurus did things according to their inner truth. They paid little heed to social conditioning and conduct. Social conditioning told us that we had to act a certain way, even if we felt differently inside so that we could fit into a system. The trouble with that was that it ignored our feelings and the longings of our soul. Gurus knew this, and shattered our belief systems at every turn. So in other words, a guru could actually look like the average asshole to you, because they didn't act in accordance to societies' expectations.

Namadeva strummed his Tambura and chanted. He truly enjoyed his work, and I could never imagine him being harsh or arrogant in any way. At one point in the seminar he bowed to Arathi Ma and said, "Thank you for coming, Arathi. Humility is the greatest attribute." No one's heart was safe from Namadeva's consideration, and his beautiful nature empowered me to pursue my mantra practice with greater fervor.

Monday, after the weekend was finished, Namadeva gave individual consultations. His rates were more than reasonable, but I didn't have enough money to book a session with him. It saddened me because I longed to be in his presence. I really didn't care what advice he had to give, although I'm sure that it would have been most valuable.

That night, I was proven of Namadeva's greatness. He came to me in a dream, his hands gesturing in various patterns. Symbols manifested before him and flew straight into my forehead. He had initiated me into some energy. I guessed that it was the great Gayatri Mantra, the main staple of his forty-year discipline.

Months later, Jamie and I attended one of his Puja ceremonies in Oregon State. I was excited to see him, and the ceremony was most powerful. I will remember it always because it was the last time I saw him before he passed away, but I'm sure that his soul is still with us. I dream of him from time to time, and I'm sure that there are thousands of people that do so as well.

Namadeva will always be in my prayers, not only for what he taught, but for *how* he taught it. I encourage everyone to read or listen to his works; they will change your life.

Miracles

Soon the time came for me to leave the dealership. Like I said, I wasn't much of a salesperson, and the money was clearly reflecting it. I decided to count my blessings and leave, knowing that one day the lessons in such a venture would be revealed to me.

Working there was not a total loss. For one thing, working at a dealership with little or no customers had given me an abundance of Facebook time. I'd post the newest of our used cars online and pray that someone in my friend's list would respond to the ads. Perhaps they had a friend of a friend of a friend that needed a car. I got little or no bites on the ads, so I then resigned my time to reconnecting with old friends.

During my tour of duty at the dealership, I had managed to reconnect with a couple that I had known years earlier. George had been running natural bodybuilding contests for over ten years, and I had competed in the very first show he had run. George and his wife, Janet, were still running bodybuilding and fitness contests, but due to a few setbacks, they were struggling to find their new place in the fitness industry. They had lost their house and their empire because of a series of unlucky and costly events, and were forced to move into Janet's family's summer cottage. Her parents had been graceful enough to allow her and George to live there until they got back onto their feet. Things were not going well at all. I did know however, that happiness could exist in spite of all their bad luck.

In my conversation with them, I mentioned what the last few years of my life had entailed and some of things that I had learned. I taught them a few mantras that might help with their abundance challenges and then proceeded to keep in touch with a phone call or email every few weeks.

Soon enough, they booked several Skype consultations with Arathi Ma (they lived too far away to meet in person). After experiencing some success, George and Janet then decided that they would like to work with Arathi Ma in person.

George and Janet invited us to their cottage, and I figured that perhaps this was an opportunity for Arathi Ma and I to see how I could assist in a larger way with her work. After all, I had been studying with her for over two years. She had observed that I had a keen sense of truth and a way of explaining her techniques from a different perspective. Perhaps I could find a way to be of service to George and Janet.

George picked us up from the airport in his rental car -- because he didn't have a car of his own -- and although he was happy to see us, his mood was not as cheerful as I would have expected. The reunion at the airport had not been the reunion of long lost friends, but the aloof meeting of those engaged in serious business. I did sense the old, jovial George underneath all the seriousness, but the stresses of life had squeezed the happiness right out of him.

We pulled into the forested driveway of the summer cottage and were met by three barking dogs. Janet greeted us at the front door, but her expression was also devoid of the natural ease of friendship. There was grief and terror in her eyes, and it had probably been there for so long, I doubt she was even aware of it.

I decided that Arathi Ma's energy had already been working with them. They were already cleansing whatever emotional patterns impeded their happiness.

I had seen it in Arathi Ma's students before. Upon signing up for a six-hour workshop, her students' emotional issues would come out in a storm throughout the day. I sometimes could relate them to a bunch of preschoolers that had gone without their afternoon nap. I, of course, was included in this group. The only difference was that I was in a constant flux between tired preschooler and colicky infant…and this moodiness pretty much went on twenty-four seven. I am proud to admit that I have moved beyond the initial stages evolution, however. Although I am incapable of playing well with others, I am quite proficient at putting on my own pants – sometimes backwards -- and combing my hair. And, with some success, I have continued to work on the other big boy stuff along my journey.

Arathi Ma and I were scheduled to stay with George and Janet for a week. The summer weather was beautiful and hot, but that wasn't the only heat that George and Janet were experiencing. Judging by their demeanors, Arathi Ma's fire was cooking them as well -- as it had nicely seared my backside for the last two years.

What am I saying? My backside wasn't seared. It was slapped, cooked, burnt, and then thrown into a volcano. If I survive it, I'll tell you how it ends up.

We were not at the cottage long before we got started with our work. Arathi Ma started a question and answer period with them and I observed her like I always did…with fascination. She knew how consciousness moved, how it worked, and it became quite obvious that consciousness was involved in everything. In only a few hours, Arathi Ma unraveled that the true problems were not from the couple's business, but from the issues surrounding relationships and the traumas of their past.

Not only were George and Janet not able to connect to the people in their business lives, but their relationships with their families and each other were struggling as well. In the midst of their pain, they had done what so many others had done before them; they shut off their feelings entirely. It was no wonder that their past relationships were strewn with disloyalty; George and Janet were incapable of showing their feelings to the people they cared about.

Arathi Ma immediately started them on exercises that would help them feel their energetic system again. She taught them how to face each other and connect their chakras. It became clear that George was unable to open or connect his second chakra. If he didn't learn to do so, intimacy or passion in his life would be impossible. Interestingly enough, Janet had similar problems with her own second chakra.

From there, Arathi Ma orchestrated more energetic exercises and she encountered resistance along the way. George and Janet had buried parts of themselves deep inside and were reluctant to rediscover them again.

They were moderately comfortable with their coping strategies, although it was quite apparent that the strategies caused them pain. They – like most people – wanted to change their life on the outside, but were tentative about going inside themselves to do so. As Arathi Ma had said to me, everything had to be in alignment for change to happen. Their inner selves were not congruent with their goals, so she had to get them to work on themselves first before their business needs could be met.

That night we decided to have a fire on the beach. It would give us a chance to talk in a more casual manner therefore allowing us to connect more to George and Janet. I was excited, not only for the work with them, but for the campfire. I hadn't enjoyed a fire for quite a long time and I looked forward to it with a fervor that reminded me of my childhood. As an exercise, Arathi Ma asked for George and Janet to put the pains of their past onto paper so that they could enter them into the fire. She urged them to also include their prayers on the paper so that when the fire consumed the paper, their prayers would be carried upwards to the divine.

If I had heard such a thing years before meeting Arathi Ma I would have thought that putting prayers in a fire was weird. I was surprised at how receptive George and Janet were. It seemed that they had a curiosity for the mysteries of the universe, and were quite excited about seeing what would happen. I knew then that they were kindred spirits. After all, curiosity had taken me far on my own spiritual journey.

We strolled outside and collected some wood from a woodshed beside the driveway. I learned then that although George had lived in the cabin for a year, he had swum in the lake only a few times and hadn't enjoyed a single fire. He lived in the middle of an outdoor paradise, but chose to stick himself inside in front of a computer instead. He said that work had kept him busy, but I could not see how. He was running fewer competitions than ever and his finances were proof of it. How could he be too busy to even leave the house?

Giving further proof as to George's whereabouts for the past year was his struggle to light the campfire. He built the nest of sticks, twigs, and newspaper, but the fire would not catch on the wood. It seemed fitting that he could not ignite passion for his life and he couldn't light a campfire either. He tried for several minutes, but only managed to create a small group of smoking embers. To George's credit, it probably didn't help that I hovered over his shoulder panting wildly at the prospect of enjoying the flames under the stars.

That was when Arathi Ma stepped in.

At that point even I was sobered of my familiarity with Arathi Ma. I was used to being in her presence and the spiritual phenomenon that manifested because of it. Spiritual mist, psychic abilities, and intense energetic sensations moving through my body were all casual experiences for me, but they hadn't prepared me for what I saw next.

George's repeated tries to light the fire had ended up in a small orange glow underneath a pile of timber. Arathi Ma asked George to step back, and then she raised her hands above the struggling embers.

"I call upon Shiva to give life to this fire."

Immediately, blue flames rose from the ashes to consume the wood. George and Janet gasped and looked at each other to confirm what they had just seen. I couldn't believe it either. Had it been coincidence? I also thought it odd that the flames had emerged blue in color. Anyone who saw a picture of the Hindu God Shiva would tell you that he was blue.

After our laughter and excitement from what had happened faded, my mind still worked on what had happened. Why the hell hadn't she done that before? I shook my head; there was still so much I didn't know about Arathi Ma.

The fire grew warm and bright and it had long since turned to a normal orange color. We enjoyed casual conversation while enjoying the warding ability the smoke had on the swarm of mosquitoes that buzzed around the lake, and I could not help but notice the happiness that George and Janet carried from witnessing a miracle.

Soon, George and Janet offered their list of prayers into the fire. A few minutes passed and George started wiping his baldhead.

"Is it raining?" he asked.

We all shook our heads. The night was as warm and dry as a summer night could be.

"Something cool and wet is touching my head." He cast his gaze up into the trees over us, searching for any hint of moisture.

We all noticed a sense of relaxation wash over the four of us and it reminded me of one of the blessings I had received in my apartment. Something had happened, but I didn't know what. I thought that perhaps it was a side effect of George's letter he had burned. Confusion and humor showed in his expression.

"That was weird," he said, glancing all around for the source of the cool mist.

Arathi Ma sat beside me on a stump. She ignored our conversation and her attention was turned on something behind me. I followed her gaze and saw nothing but darkness -- which started to creep me out. A dark forest is a beautiful thing...if you have fangs. At night, my mind came up with an entire assortment of Nasties lurking in the darkness.

"What is it?" I said, hoping my voice sounded manly, but knowing different. After all, this woman had just created fire. If she was nervous about something, I decided that it was best if I was too.

"There's someone back there. A Native man."

George then pointed out that the lake sat on a Native Indian Reserve. Arathi Ma didn't know this, of course, so this was yet another one of the confirmations that her psychic sense was right on.

"A Native man," I said. I turned my flashlight towards the darkened trees. "I don't see anyone."

"He's in spirit form."

"Oh."

Now I don't know about you, but I know a lot of people that would run from the forest at that point, lock themselves in a room, and rock back and forth until they wore a hole in the back of their pants. I am proud to say that I did not do this, of course, and I don't mean to brag about my bravery, but I even managed to speak under such scary circumstances. "What does he want?" After all, I was used to visitations of the souls of the living. How could visitations of the souls of the dead be much different?

"He seems shy." Arathi Ma smiled.

I used my perception to search the forest. I definitely felt something in the trees, and the more I went into the sensation, the less intimidating it became. She was right. The man felt shy, as if he didn't want to intrude on our gathering.

I decided to test if my intuition was accurate. I turned my hands upward in a greeting of humility. "Please, if you are really here watching us, then give us a sign of your presence."

I saw a flitting of movement in the corner of my eye. It came from amid the embers of the fire. I couldn't believe it. A small frog emerged right from the cinders. "Where did that come from?"

Arathi Ma laughed. "He came from the fire. You saw it, didn't you?"

I had, but I couldn't believe it. I tried to logically explain it to myself. Perhaps the frog had buried himself in the sandy fire pit before we had built a fire over top of him, but I still couldn't ignore that even if that was true, why did the frog hop to my feet exactly when my prayer had finished?

I loved that frog. He was a sign of the divine at work. I wanted to pick him up. I moved to do so, when Arathi Ma grabbed my arm and said, "No. It might kill him.'

"I just wanted to pick him up. I'm not going to hurt him."

Arathi Ma patted my arm. "I know, but the Native's spirit moved through the frog to give you a sign. He controlled the frog to do it and it puts the animal through a certain amount of stress. You have received the sign and that is good enough."

I remembered a story that I had read in "Autobiography of a Yogi." In this particular story the main character's guru had actually mind-controlled a man. He had done it so thoroughly that he had utterly controlled the man's every action. I understood then that perhaps the Natives had experimented with this power as well and could use it on animals.

I stared up at the stars and thanked the Native spirit for his sign. Arathi Ma had started a fire with a prayer and had been a catalyst in the magical appearance of a frog from the same fire. Two things I had thought impossible.

Nothing was ever boring around Arathi Ma.

Saved by a Dragonfly

Everyday at the cabin we'd wake up to sound of barking dogs, manage a quick breakfast, and then we'd rush out the door like two kids on summer vacation. We'd enjoy our mornings by jumping off the dock into the lake and swimming in the dark and forbidding water. Don't get me wrong, the lake was beautiful, but due to its mineral content, the water took on a brown color and it was impossible to see more than a few feet past the surface.

One day, after we grew tired from swimming, Arathi Ma and I rendezvoused on the dock to discuss George and Janet's progress.

There had been numerous signs of improvement. George and Janet smiled often and were more at ease with their situation. There had been numerous synchronistic events behind their new shift in happiness as well.

In one meeting, George and Janet told Arathi Ma that they were having trouble with finding the right person for a position in their company. Several months had passed in their search with little success. Arathi Ma's first step was to help them release the emotional pain around the last person that had held the position. After that was finished, she cleared their conflicting motives around filling the position and what it meant in the structure of their new idea of fulfillment in their lives. Did they really need a person in this position? What were their bigger goals and was their structure clearly reflecting them? To get the answers to these questions, Arathi Ma had to help them release their demons of the past so that they could properly deal with the moment at hand. After long hours of debate and energetic correction, George received a call from a man the next day. The man had heard about the available position and wished to apply for it.

The shock on George's face was evident. He could not believe that the energetic exercises had produced such a quick result. I was more surprised than he was. I was used to using spiritual energy to improve my life, but it seemed that the divine never gave me what I asked for, but what I needed instead. What could I say? I guessed the divine knew that I wasn't smart enough to micromanage my life.

It seemed that George and Janet experienced something different altogether.

On another occasion, Arathi Ma urged me to perform some energetic healing on Janet. I felt a blockage in her second chakra, so I proceeded to energetically power wash the area. It was then that Janet started to feel something happening in her throat. The throat chakra, in part, stood for self-expression. Was there something that she wished to express to the world? I knew that Janet felt guilty about losing her dowry to her bankrupt business. After all, her parents had given it to her so that she could start a family, not risk it on a business venture. I also knew that slowly over time, because of the guilt, Janet had disconnected real communication with her parents so that she didn't have to inform them of the full ramifications of her financial situation. Perhaps Janet's blockages in her chakras had stemmed from her fear of telling her parents the truth.

The next day, I received a sign that the healing had taken effect. After experiencing the sensation in her throat, Janet decided to call her parents and tell them everything that had happened. After having a heart-felt conversation with her family, she was surprised to find out how understanding they were. Her mood brightened beyond description.

I started to see that life wasn't as much a journey, but a constant letting go of our past experiences. When Janet told her family what had happened, she was able to let go of a painful part of her past. This enabled her to move forward again with the wisdom that her experiences had taught her.

Arathi Ma knew no bounds when it came to healing. Not only were George and Janet not safe from her magical skills, the dogs weren't either. One black, curly-haired dog, Buster, was a funny sort of fellow. He'd constantly stare about the room and nip at the air. Sometimes he aimed his chomps at flies, but we noticed that sometimes his snaps were at nothing at all. I often wondered if Buster was a dog that could see energy or ghosts. Maybe he'd incarnate in a subsequent life as the next Sylvia Brown.

Well, besides his little hobbies, Buster had one small flaw. If anyone touched his tail, he'd snarl like a wild, pack animal. If one was unlucky enough to even brush by it, they were likely to get bitten. Now, that was uncharacteristic of Buster because he was a lovely, gentle dog. He didn't bark too much and responded well to affection. I would say that he was perfect, except for his little problem.

One day, Buster exhibited his behavior to Janet. She walked by him and her leg accidentally brushed his backside. He turned on her in a wild snarl, but didn't bite her. Buster moped about after that, and it was obvious that he was not happy about the entire incident. I almost sensed that he felt guilt from his overzealous reaction.

This caught Arathi Ma's attention. She glided over to the dog and placed her hand on his back. She then closed her eyes and started communicating with him. Her head turned back and forth as she scanned the information that came to her.

Her eyes still closed, Arathi Ma said, "He was hurt when he was a puppy. Did someone step on him? Not just his tail, but he was really hurt, right?"

Janet nodded. "The mailman stepped on him. We had to take him to the vet. It was pretty bad."

I noticed then that Arathi Ma's hand had made its way to Buster's tail. She touched it gently and Buster didn't move an inch. Then her voice came in a soothing whisper, telling him that it would be okay.

The next day, Janet and Buster shared the couch. And Janet absentmindedly petted his backside.

I pointed it out to her. "Holy crap! You couldn't do that before."

Janet laughed. "Oh yeah. That's amazing."

Janet and George's lives had changed for the better, but their lives weren't the only ones that were affected. As the days wore on, my role with Arathi Ma became clearer. I taught what I knew, but where I truly served was in assisting in driving home Arathi Ma's complex teachings. The truth of the matter was that the teachings were really simple…when observed from the right perspective, and that's where I came in. I came up with metaphor after metaphor to explain Arathi Ma's words from as many different angles as possible and then inevitably the light would go on in either Janet or George's head.

One night, I went out on the dock with Arathi Ma to see the stars. We were happy with our success in our work and it added to our enjoyment of a truly beautiful place. Frogs croaked and the odd Loon called in the distance. There was something different about this lake in the way it felt. I expressed this to Arathi Ma.

She said, "This lake sits on a solid foundation of rock, so it is better for grounding energy."

My energy had been quite active since arriving to the cottage. Visions came to me with greater frequency during my meditations and I guess that it must have had something to do with the land. Another thought came to mind.

"You've done readings and healings on me back home, but I've never seen you do the fire thing. Is your power greater here or something? Or have you just been holding out on me?" I suspected the latter.

Arathi Ma laughed and played coy. "The opportunity never came up before."

"You could've used your power to light the candles in our apartment."

"And what if I accidentally lit the entire building on fire?"

"I'd be willing to risk it, if it meant the fire took the Dog Mat with it." The echoes of our laughter could be heard far across the lake that night. "Really, why didn't you show me these miracles before?"

Arathi Ma thought for a moment. "And how would I pick which miracle to show. The universe is a miracle. The fact that you and I can speak to each other is a miracle. It is just your mind that wants to delineate between which feat is a miracle and which is not. The truth is that *everything* is a miracle." She thought for a moment. "Besides this power is not my own. The divine works through me at the right time. I cannot will it to happen. It only works through me when it is called to."

"So it's kind of like the Ego thing. All doing happens through the Ego. True power from the divine cannot come from that place; it can only come from a place of being."

Arathi Ma smiled and gave me a hug. "Yup." She was using her usual diversionary tactic when our conversation got too engaged in the questions of the mind.

"What about--"

Arathi hugged me harder and then swung from my shoulders like a child. "Love's all that matters."

After embracing for a few moments, she bid me good night. She started back towards the house, but what I saw was unbelievable.

"Wait a minute," I said.

She turned. "Yes."

There was a tunnel of translucent energy shooting upwards from her head. It was a foot wide and resembled the cloaking device that the invisible monster wore in the movie Predator. I moved from side to side, checking if my eyes were playing tricks on me, but the energy remained, warping whatever lay behind it.

"My crown chakra is open, isn't it?" Arathi Ma smiled.

"Is that what that is?"

She nodded. "When it's open, it's easier to see the spiritual energy that comes out of it."

Arathi Ma waited patiently for me to walk all the way around her and I decided that without a doubt the energy was not a trick of the eyes. The night stars appeared distorted when I looked through the energy tube above her head, and then they visibly cleared as soon as I looked at them from a different angle.

"Is it ever going to stop?" I said.

"What do you mean?"

"It seems that every time I think I've experienced everything, something knew happens."

Arathi Ma laughed. "That's the great part about the spiritual life. It never stays the same. No moment is the same. Boredom does not exist when you're in your core. Do you see what I'm saying?"

I nodded, my eyes scanning the beam of translucence above her head. "I'm starting to." A smile came to my lips. I had struggled with boredom my entire life and I had thought that it was merely a reality that I had to deal with. It was a terrible relief to receive another confirmation that my former theory wasn't true.

The next day, Arathi Ma and I decided to go for a ride around the lake in a pedal boat. We threw the boat into the water, sat in it, and were off like two pirates out to storm the seven seas. We had high aspirations, but the lake was much bigger than we thought. It was complete with forested islands and the lake was littered water skiers and boats. We paddled for a good thirty minutes and decided that traversing the waves wasn't as relaxing as it had first appeared. My legs burned with fatigue and I was sure that Arathi Ma was tired as well.

It was time to turn back.

It didn't take long before I discovered why I had tired so suddenly; Arathi Ma was a cheater in the pedaling department. Several times I struggled to move our little boat forward and wondered what impeded our pace. Then I'd glance over at Arathi Ma and see that her feet were clearly resting on the pedals. I should have seen it sooner; we had been chanting mantras aloud for quite some time and for some reason I was the only one out of breath.

We turned the boat around and pedaled back to the cottage (actually, I pedaled back, and only received intermittent assistance from Arathi Ma when I glared in her direction).

I soon came to the realization that I had made a wrong turn in Timbuktu.

The trip had been a half an hour in one direction and close to an hour back. I had clearly lost my way, and I admit to a little embarrassment, seeing as I was the designated navigator.

I thought, what kind of idiot gets lost on a lake? That's when the buzzer sounded, and the inevitable answer of "Jason" came to me.

Finally Arathi Ma turned to me and asked the age-old question that all women ask their men at one or more times in their life. "Are you lost?"

And I responded with the age-old response of many men before me. "No."

Of course, I couldn't out smart or lie to Arathi Ma…for long.

"You're lost," she said.

"Okay fine, I'm lost, but I don't see any gas stations around here to buy a map."

She turned in the boat, searching for her bearings. "I think we're back that way."

"I don't think so." Maybe I was wrong, but that didn't mean I wanted to admit it.

"Yes, we are."

Arathi Ma grabbed the steering handle and turned us around.

"How can you be sure?" I rambled off a series of reasons why we were already heading in the right direction. She wasn't buying any of it.

"I'm not sure where we are, but something doesn't feel right. I'm going to call in some help."

I glanced around the lake. "I don't see a tow truck anywhere. Where's the help going come from?"

Arathi Ma turned her palms upward and raised her hands. "I call upon a dragonfly to guide us home."

I laughed. "Nice try." There were dragonflies all around the lake, but I was sure one wasn't going to pull out a map and give us directions.

A minute passed and then the largest dragonfly I had ever seen landed on my leg.

Arathi Ma laughed. "Thank you for coming," she said.

I started to pedal our boat and all the while the dragonfly clung to my leg. Upon several occasions, I expected it to fly away with the up and down movement of my leg, but it seemed content, almost as if it was enjoying the ride.

Arathi Ma laughed again. "Lead us home, little one. Stay on his leg if we're going in the right direction and then show us which bay to turn into so that we can go home."

I pedaled and watched the dragonfly. Disbelief consumed me. One minute passed. Then two. Before I knew it, approximately four minutes passed before the dragonfly leapt into the air and flew thirty feet straight ahead. It then took a sharp right into the nearest bay.

And just like Arathi Ma had requested, in that bay, our cabin waited for us.

I shook my head in disbelief. "Now when did you learn to do that?"

Soon the day came for us to leave Janet and George. Arathi Ma's work had changed their lives forever. And the life of their dog, Buster, too. Their good byes were filled with honesty and connection. No longer were their smiles hiding the pains of the past underneath. They had achieved a victory on the road of life.

I wish them well in all their endeavors.

The Awakening

Arathi Ma and I returned to Vancouver and daily life with resumed. I was out of a job, so I assisted her with her workshops and meditations instead. I continued my spiritual sadhana as I always had, chanting mantras day and night. My mala went everywhere I went, and I often got it caught in doors, on buttons, and any other object you can imagine. I had figured out that it wasn't the chanting of the mantras that was so difficult, it was the keeping track of them that was the problem.

One day, as I sat on my chair beside the Dog Mat, I felt a light fluffy feeling move through my entire body. It suddenly felt like there was little difference between my skin and the environment around me, almost as if I had become more at one with it. My old shoulder injury, which usually nagged at me often, melted away. My shoulder no longer felt uncomfortable or out of place in any way. The same sensation flowed through my back and legs and I decided that I must have hit the one hundred and thirty thousand repetition mark of one of the many mantras I practiced.

I went the gym that day and enjoyed the greatest workout I had had in a long time. My shoulder was more efficient in its motion. I no longer was in constant worry about whether it was going to dislocate (although I'm sure that it would have if I risked an extreme throwing motion).

A few weeks after the sensation of the new energy in my body, I woke up to another day of spiritual cleansing. The Soup de Jour was irritation. I was irritated at everything. Not in the extreme sense, but for some reason the world seemed more difficult than usual.

Like a panther on the hunt, Arathi Ma stalked into the room in anticipation of another emotional kill. As a Guru she was a master at hunting out the "non truths" that surfaced from my spiritual disciplines.

"A little off today, eh?" Arathi Ma said.

I don't know about you, but when I'm in a bad mood and someone tells me I'm in a bad mood or that I'm "off," I feel like throwing something at them. Of course I could never do that to Arathi Ma, even though she was a master of dancing on my nerves when I least wanted it. That was how she purged my patterns to the surface.

I suppressed as much of my bad mood as I could and gave her a simple answer.

"Irritated and bored. Another cleanse, I guess."

I didn't like the feeling of irritation, but I was also aware that the mood wasn't me. The cleanse was just another side effect of my mantra practice and being in the burning radius of Arathi Ma's fire.

Arathi Ma motioned for me to sit and then held her hands above my stomach. She gazed into my eyes for a few minutes, as if conducting an inner conversation with my soul. All the while, she transmitted energy into me through her hands. I felt some of my irritation leave. I guess you could call her an energetic leaf blower. I had a lot of leaves falling off my inner tree and she helped with the cleanup work.

Actually, that wasn't entirely accurate.

Arathi Ma not only helped with cleaning up the leaves, but she took a chainsaw to the branches of my tree from time to time.

After a minute of the work, Arathi Ma said, "That irritation is from your childhood. You need to let that go." Arathi Ma then promptly left to take a shower, leaving me by myself.

I heard the shower start – after all, the bathroom was only ten feet away from me – and then the room started to morph and change.

Somehow everything in the room appeared the same, but my judgment of distance and time became warped. A picture of Ganapathi sat on the bookshelf. I stared at it and an incredible peace moved through me. Then I became conscious of an immense tickle in my chest.

What is that? I thought.

That was when the laughter started. It was subtle at first, but became more intense. I wasn't sure what I was laughing at. Actually, I knew that I wasn't laughing at anything at all, which made the situation all the funnier. I laughed and laughed, waves of incredible peace and infinity moving through me. I suddenly understood that there was no such thing as time – not in the way we thought of it. That the only moment that existed was now. The now was too infinite to contemplate, so how could anyone even think about the past or the future. From another perspective, I remember feeling like time and distance were related in some way. It made sense to me; it took time to travel anywhere so how could time and distance not be related?

I moved to the balcony and stared at the sky. For hours I sat without a single care in the world. How could I worry about anything in the presence of such incredible peace? I knew that without a doubt that this was enlightenment.

What an incredible experience, I thought. If only I could maintain it.

And I guess that was where the difference was. An Awakened person has had the experience of enlightenment. Perhaps an enlightened person could hold it and make it permanent.

Every spiritual experience I had had changed how I thought of the world, but the Awakening's effect on me was much more profound. Part of who I thought I was, my identity, had died that day. Not only had it died, I forgot it entirely. It was like some part of myself that had played such an integral role in who I was left completely and didn't leave a going away note.

I was more of what I truly was without a thought or idea of it. Spiritual experiences were no longer my highest aspiration, my state of being was. In the new state, my entire life became a spiritual experience. Every breath, every step.

I moved forward with new perspective. Why perceive the Universe when I could become it. Some major part of me had moved toward this new way of being and I knew that my evolution wasn't finished yet.

Epilogue

Since the day of my Awakening, I was never the same. Daily activities continued in much the same way as they had before, but the feelings behind everything ran deeper inside me. I felt raw in the world, as if my thoughts had somehow faded to the background so that my feelings could emerge to the forefront.

Of course my mind would reemerge with thoughts and commentary from time to time, but when the thoughts caused me suffering, I could easily push them aside and readjust myself so that I remained in the now. I had become a master of some part of my intellectual self. I had disempowered my identification with my thoughts and not only could I choose to disregard them entirely, but I could actually turn off my thoughts whenever I chose.

For years I had walked around with thoughts constantly buzzing inside my head. They told me to do this or that because if I didn't, something bad was going to happen. My mind had told me that it was perfectly logical to worry about a problem that I had no solution to, as if worrying would somehow bring solutions to life's difficulties.

I was free from all of it. If my mind wandered into the problems of the past in order to connect them to the present, I could merely sever the cord between them. The moment became new, fresh. New problems required new solutions. No longer did an obstacle mean a shopping list of memories or past traumas that held little relevance to the present.

The major side effect of all of it was that I experienced extreme pleasure and happiness with greater regularity. I felt everything in a much deeper way. Colors became a kaleidoscope of emotions for me and I was known to shed more than one tear of joy when watching cartoons. Sometimes colors or smells took me back to the early days of my childhood. Not only did they bring memories flooding back, but I could immediately feel exactly how I had felt upon first experiencing such stimulus as a boy. It was as if I was able to re-experience the first joyful moments of my life over and over again. And each time I did, I was surprised at how I had totally forgotten the overpowering emotions that had gone with those first experiences.

I cannot adequately explain the sheer level of physical bliss and ecstasy that I enjoyed. The softest of breezes would send light fluffy feelings through my body. Meditations brought a myriad of different physical sensations beyond anything that I had felt before. It was if parts of my body that had long since died were resurrected from death. Once I was free from the mind, the world became a place of pleasure.

And after months of enjoying this new state of being, my next journey began...

Those wishing to contact Jason Gallant may do so at:

www.jasongallant.ca

Those wishing to contact Arathi Ma may do so at:

www.seedsoflife.ca